First World War
and Army of Occupation
War Diary
France, Belgium and Germany

32 DIVISION
97 Infantry Brigade
Manchester Regiment
51st (G) Battalion
15 March 1919 - 31 October 1919

WO95/2404/1

The Naval & Military Press Ltd
www.nmarchive.com
Published in association with The National Archives

Published by

The Naval & Military Press Ltd

Unit 10 Ridgewood Industrial Park,

Uckfield, East Sussex,

TN22 5QE England

Tel: +44 (0) 1825 749494

www.naval-military-press.com

www.nmarchive.com

This diary has been reprinted in facsimile from the original. Any imperfections are inevitably reproduced and the quality may fall short of modern type and cartographic standards.

© **Crown Copyright**
Images reproduced by permission of The National Archives, London, England, 2015.

Contents

Document type	Place/Title	Date From	Date To
Heading	WO95/2404/1		
Heading	Lancashire Division (Late 32nd Divn) 97th Infy Bde (3rd Lancs Infy Bde) 51st Bn Manchester Regt Mar-Oct 1919		
Heading	51st Bn Manchester Regt. C 424 Of 7th /4/19 War Diary March 1919 Vol I		
War Diary	Dover	15/03/1919	15/03/1919
War Diary	Dunkirk	16/03/1919	18/03/1919
War Diary	Bonn	19/03/1919	30/03/1919
War Diary	Siegburg Muldorf	31/03/1919	31/03/1919
Miscellaneous	Extract From Battalion Order No. 60 Dated March 13th		
Heading	War Diary Of 51st Bn. Manchester Regt April 1919		
War Diary	Seig Burg Muldorf	01/04/1919	02/04/1919
War Diary	Birlinghoven	03/04/1919	30/04/1919
Miscellaneous	Training Programme For Week Ending April 18th 1919	11/04/1919	11/04/1919
Miscellaneous	Programme Of Educational Training For W.E. April 10th 1919 Appendix "B"	10/04/1919	10/04/1919
Miscellaneous	Sports Programme For Week Ending April 18th 1919 Appendix C	18/04/1919	18/04/1919
Miscellaneous	Training Programe For Week Ending April 16th 1919	16/04/1919	16/04/1919
Miscellaneous	Programme Of Educational Training For Week Ending April 26th 1919	26/04/1919	26/04/1919
Miscellaneous	Education Training Programe	17/04/1919	17/04/1919
Miscellaneous	Sports Programme For Week Ending April 26th 1919	26/04/1919	26/04/1919
War Diary	Birlinghoven	01/05/1919	31/05/1919
Miscellaneous	51st Bn The Manchester Regiment "G" Training For Week Ending May 2nd 1919	24/04/1919	24/04/1919
Miscellaneous	51st Bn The Manchester Regiment Training Programme For Week Ending May 3rd 1919	24/04/1919	24/04/1919
Miscellaneous	51st Bn The Manchester Regiment	25/04/1919	25/04/1919
Miscellaneous	51st Bn The Manchester Regiment Programme Of Educational Training For W/E May 3rd 1919	24/04/1919	24/04/1919
Miscellaneous	51st Bn The Manchester Regiment	25/04/1919	25/04/1919
Miscellaneous	51st Bn The Manchester Regiment Programme Of Educational Training For W/E May 3rd 1919	24/04/1919	24/04/1919
Miscellaneous	51st Bn The Manchester Regiment Sports Programme For Week Ending May 10th 1919	10/05/1919	10/05/1919
Miscellaneous	51st Bn The Manchester Regiment Programme Of Educational Training For Week Ending May 10th 1919	10/05/1919	10/05/1919
Miscellaneous	Education Programme Continued for W.E May 10th. 1919	30/04/1919	30/04/1919
Miscellaneous	51st Bn The Manchester Regiment Sport Programme For Week Ending May 18th 1919	08/05/1919	08/05/1919
Miscellaneous	51st Bn The Manchester Regiment Programme Of Educational Training For Week Ending 17th 1919	17/05/1919	17/05/1919
Miscellaneous	51st Bn The Manchester Regiment		
Miscellaneous	51st Bn The Manchester Regiment Training Programme For Week Ending May 24th 1919	16/05/1919	16/05/1919
Miscellaneous	51st Bn The Manchester Regiment Programme Of Educational Training For Week Ending May 24th 1919	15/05/1919	15/05/1919

Miscellaneous	51st Bn The Manchester Regiment Sports Programme For Week Ending May 31st 1919	23/05/1919	23/05/1919
Miscellaneous	51st Bn The Manchester Regiment Of Educational Training For Week Ending May 31st 1919	31/05/1919	31/05/1919
War Diary	Birlinghoven	01/06/1919	18/06/1919
War Diary	Dambroich	19/06/1919	30/06/1919
Operation(al) Order(s)	51st Battalion Manchester Regt. Operation Order No. 1	01/06/1919	01/06/1919
Operation(al) Order(s)	51st Battalion Manchester Regt. Operation Order No. 2		
Operation(al) Order(s)	51st Battalion Manchester Regt. Operation Order No. 3		
Miscellaneous	51st Bn Manchester Regiment Proposed Programme Of Training For Week Ending June 21st 1919	13/06/1919	13/06/1919
Miscellaneous	51st Bn Manchester Regiment Programme Of Educational Training For Week Ending June 21st 1919	11/06/1919	11/06/1919
Miscellaneous	Return Of Regiment Officers Entitled To Temporary Rank.		
Miscellaneous	51st Bn Manchester Regiment Programme For Week Ending June 21st 1919	02/06/1919	02/06/1919
Miscellaneous	Daily Orders Part II.	31/03/1919	31/03/1919
Miscellaneous	Boxing At Rauschendorf		
Miscellaneous	Athletic Sports at Birlinghoven.		
Miscellaneous	Programme Of Education For Week Ending	26/06/1919	26/06/1919
Operation(al) Order(s)	51st Bn. The Manchester Regiment Operation Order No. 4	27/06/1919	27/06/1919
War Diary	Birlinghoven	01/07/1919	01/07/1919
War Diary	Menden	02/07/1919	31/07/1919
Miscellaneous	51st Battn, The Manchester Regiment Battalion Concert.		
Miscellaneous	51st Bn Manchester Regiment Sports Programme Week Ending July 19th 1919		
Miscellaneous	51st Bn Manchester Regiment Programme Of Educational Training For Week Ending July 12th 1919		
Miscellaneous	51st Bn Manchester Regiment Sports Programme For Week Ending July 13th 1919	05/07/1919	05/07/1919
Miscellaneous	51st Battn, The Manchester Regiment Programme of Educational Training for the Week ending July 26/?		
Miscellaneous	Sports Programme For Week-Ending 27-6-1919		
Miscellaneous	51st Bn Manchester Regiment Sports Programme For Week Ending August 3rd 1919	24/07/1919	24/07/1919
Miscellaneous	51st Bn. The Manchester Regiment Programme Of Training For Week Ending 2/8/19	23/07/1919	23/07/1919
Miscellaneous	51st Bn Manchester Regiment Programme Of Training For Week Ending July 13th 1919		
Miscellaneous	Programme	07/07/1919	07/07/1919
Miscellaneous	51st Bn Manchester Regiment Programme Of Training For Week Ending July 19th 1919		
Miscellaneous	51st Bn Manchester Regiment Programme Of Educational For Week Ending July 19th 1919	10/07/1919	10/07/1919
Miscellaneous	51st Bn Manchester Regiment Programme Of Training For Week Ending July 26th 1919	26/07/1919	26/07/1919
Miscellaneous	51st Bn. The Manchester Regiment Programme Of Training For Week Ending August 2nd, 1919	26/07/1919	26/07/1919
War Diary	Menden	01/08/1919	05/08/1919
War Diary	Geistingen	06/08/1919	31/08/1919
Miscellaneous	Programme Of Training For Week Ending August 9th, 1919	01/08/1919	01/08/1919
Miscellaneous	Sports Programme For Week Ending 10th August 1919	01/08/1919	01/08/1919

Miscellaneous	Programme Of Education Training For Week Ending August 9th, 1919		
Miscellaneous	N.C. O's Class Programme For Week Ending 16th August, 1919		
Miscellaneous	Proposed Programme Of Training For Week Ending 16/8/19	09/08/1919	09/08/1919
Miscellaneous	Sports Programme For Week Ending 16th. August 1919	09/08/1919	09/08/1919
Miscellaneous	Programme Of Education Training For Week Ending August 16th 1919		
Miscellaneous	Programme Of Training For Week Ending August 23rd 1919	15/08/1919	15/08/1919
Miscellaneous	N. C. O's Class Programme For Week Ending 23rd August, 1919		
Miscellaneous	Sports Programme For Week Ending 23rd August 1919		
Miscellaneous	Programme Of Education Training For Week Ending 23rd August 1919	15/08/1919	15/08/1919
Miscellaneous	Programme Of Educational Training For Week Ending 30-8-1919	21/08/1919	21/08/1919
War Diary		01/09/1919	09/09/1919
War Diary	Menden	10/09/1919	30/09/1919
Miscellaneous	Programme Of Training For Week Ending Sept. 6th 1919	20/08/1919	20/08/1919
Miscellaneous	1st Bn. The Manchester Regiment	30/08/1919	30/08/1919
Miscellaneous	Lancashire Division	09/09/1919	09/09/1919
Miscellaneous	Programme Of Educational Training For Week Ending 6th September 1919	27/08/1919	27/08/1919
Miscellaneous	Sports Programme For Week Ending 13th September		
Miscellaneous	Training Programme For Week-Ending Sept. 13th 1919	13/09/1919	13/09/1919
Miscellaneous	Programme Of Educational Training For Week Ending 13th, September 1919		
Miscellaneous	Training Programme For Week Ending September 20th 1919	11/09/1919	11/09/1919
Miscellaneous	Sports Programme For Week Ending September 20th 1919	11/09/1919	11/09/1919
Miscellaneous	Programme Of Educational Training For Week Ending 20th Sept. 1919	12/08/1919	12/08/1919
Miscellaneous	Burgermeister, Menden	12/09/1919	12/09/1919
Miscellaneous	The Burgermeister, Menden	13/09/1919	13/09/1919
Miscellaneous	Training Programme For Week Ending 27-9-19	27/09/1919	27/09/1919
Miscellaneous	Programme Of Education For Week Ending September 27th 1919	00/09/1919	00/09/1919
Miscellaneous	Sport Programme For Week Ending 28-9-19	20/09/1919	20/09/1919
Miscellaneous	Re-Organization		
Miscellaneous	Orders In The Event Of A Disturbance In The Area.		
Miscellaneous	Revised Education Programme For Weekending September 27th 1919	22/09/1919	22/09/1919
Miscellaneous	Sports Programme For Week Ending October 5th 1919	27/09/1919	27/09/1919
Miscellaneous	Programme Of Educational Training For Week Ending Oct. 4th 1919	23/09/1919	23/09/1919
War Diary	Menden	01/10/1919	31/10/1919
Miscellaneous	Training Programme For Week Ending 4th October 1919		
Miscellaneous	Training Programme For Week Ending October 12th 1919	05/10/1919	05/10/1919
Miscellaneous	Sports Programme For Week Ending October 12th 1919	03/10/1919	03/10/1919

Miscellaneous	Programme Of Educational Training For Week Ending 11th. October 19	00/10/1919	00/10/1919
Miscellaneous	Training Programme For Week Ending October 18th 1919	10/10/1919	10/10/1919
Miscellaneous	Sports Programme For Week Ending October 19th 1919	10/10/1919	10/10/1919
Miscellaneous	Programme Of Education For W/E October 18th 1919	10/10/1919	10/10/1919
Miscellaneous	Programme Of Training For Week Ending October 25th 1919	00/10/1919	00/10/1919
Miscellaneous	Sports Programme For Week Ending 25-10-19	17/10/1919	17/10/1919
Miscellaneous	Programme Of Educational Training For Weekending 25th October 1919	16/10/1919	16/10/1919
Miscellaneous	Training Programme For Week Ending 1st November 1919	24/10/1919	24/10/1919
Miscellaneous	Sports Programme For Week Ending 2nd November 1919	24/10/1919	24/10/1919
Miscellaneous	Programme Of Educational Training For Week Ending Nov. 1st 1919	00/10/1919	00/10/1919

WO95/24604/1

LANCASHIRE DIVISION
(LATE 32ND DIVN)

97TH INFY BDE (3RD LANCS INFY BDE)

1/51ST BN MANCHESTER REGT

MAR-OCT 1919

CONFIDENTIAL.

Vol I

51st Bn. Manchester Regt.

6424 of 7th 4/19.

WAR DIARY.

MARCH. 1919.

Army Form C. 2118.

WAR DIARY
or
INTELLIGENCE SUMMARY.
(Erase heading not required.)

51st Bn MANCHESTER REGT.

Instructions regarding War Diaries and Intelligence Summaries are contained in F.S. Regs., Part II and the Staff Manual respectively. Title pages will be prepared in manuscript.

Hour, Date, Place	Summary of Events and Information	Remarks and references to Appendices
15/3/19. DOVER	The Battn embarked per S.S. "PRINCESS ELIZABETH" for service with the Army of Occupation on the RHINE, and disembarked at DUNKIRK the same day. Strength of Battn 43 Officers 942 Rank & File. No transport vehicles or animals accompanied the Battn.	See Appendix I. (A).
16/3/19. to 18/3/19 DUNKIRK	Entrained for BONN on the afternoon of the 16th, and after spending those of 17th on train journey, arrived at BONN STATION on morning of 18th March.	[a?]
19/3/19 BONN	The Battn took over the ARTILLERIE CASERNE, RHEINDORFER STRASSE from the 2-A Bn Manchester Regt. MAJOR J.L. MURPHY Capt. A.C. PARKER. R.A.M.C., LT. & Q.M. J.J. BRODE, LT. F.J. COOKE LT. P.E.A. KENT, LT LAWRENCE (detached at Divl Canteen) 2/LT. H.W. BROWN and 105 rank & file of the 2-A Bn Manchester Regt have been attached for duty with the Battn. Animals + Vehicles of 2-A Manchester Regt have been taken on strength.	[a?]
20/3/19 } BONN 21/3/19 }	Guards, Fatigue + Drill Parades, Bathing. Football + Sports during afternoon.	[a?]
22/3/19 BONN	Church Parades.	

(73989) W4141—463. 400,000. 9/14. H.&J.Ltd. Forms/C. 2118/10.

WAR DIARY or **INTELLIGENCE SUMMARY.**
(Erase heading not required.)

Army Form C. 2118.

51ST. BN MANCHESTER. REGT.

Hour, Date, Place	Summary of Events and Information	Remarks and references to Appendices
23/3/19 BONN. TO 28/3/19	Drill, Skill + Guard Parades, Bathing, Football - Sports during afternoon.	(a)
29/3/19	Parades + Sports as for 28th. MAJOR KERSHAW, CAPT. C.N. HUNTER LT. J.L. GALLOWAY, 2/LT. J. PEREGRINE, 2/LT F.L. TAYLOR joined the Battn for duty. LT. F.J. COOKE and 2/LT. S.J. CRAY despatched for demobilisation. A + B Coys. left for OLINGHOVEN and STIELDORF respectively preparatory to the Battn taking over the outpost line.	(a) (a)
30/3/19 BONN	The Battn less A + B Coys. drill, still - guard parade. Football in during afternoon.	(a)
31/3/19 SIEGBURG MULDORF	The Battn took over the outpost line from the 1/5th B. BORDER REGT. after the move had been completed the disposition was as follows:- A Coy's HQ at OLINGHOVEN, + holding the whole of the Battn front not sub posts from OLINGHOVEN to FRECKWINKEL. B Coy's HQ at STIELDORF. C + D Coys and Battn HQ at SIEGBURG - MULDORF	See appendix I. (B) REF. MAP GERMANY 2L. 1/100,000 COLOGNE BRIDGEHEAD. (a)

P.C.W.[signature]
LT. COL.
Comdg. 51st B. Manchester Regt.

EXTRACT FROM BATTALION ORDER NO. 60 DATED MARCH 13TH.

CHANGE OF STATION.

The battalion will parade in full marching order to entrain at Southown station en route to the Rhine Army of Occupation. as under
RIGHT HALF BATTALION. under the C. O. consisting of officer commanding Adjutant, Messing, officer Transport officer Scout Officer Quartermaster Sig, officer Lt, T. Ffoulkes and their 8 batmen. Drummers:-23 Other ranks
"A" Company 8 officers 248 other anks
"B"   7 officers 121 other ranks.
Total 23 officers 400 other ranks.   and all baggage (20 tons)
Parade ready to move off at 0230 saty, 15th inst.
Remainder of B Coy, with 2nd, train party.

Left half battalion. under Major Wood M.C. consisting of the 2 in C A/ Adjutant Lt Huston Details B Coy, and C and D Coys. Parade ready to move off at 0310.

BAGGAGE.

All heavy baggage will be ready to load up at 0800 hrs on the 1 14th inst.
KIT BAGS are to be carried and are to be taken in the carriages with the men

they will each bear a label showing owners name etc. Coy, & Battn.

They will be stacked by Companies ready for loading at 1400 to-morrow. the 14 th inst. They will be transported to station and stacked in Company dumps on the platform Rifles must be loaded labelled as per kit bags.

PACKS.

Packs of N.C.O.s and men certified unfit to carry marching order will be put in sacks or boxes properly labelled and sent with heavy baggag

RATIONS.

Rations will be carried in bulk by Companies and dumped with Coy kit bags and loaded into the Guards van.

OFFICERS BAGGAGE.

will be packed and ready for loading by 1000 the 14tg inst.

LABELS. All ranks are warned that no compensation is admissable for kit etc lost in transit as a result of being unpropperly labelled or deficient of labels.

ORDERS FOR TROOPS.

Officers in charge of Companies will enquire that an

N.C.O. is included in each compartment. He will be held strictly responsible for the conduct of his party. No person will leave the train without the permission . All men enter the carriage and sit down with kit bags between their knees. until the compartment is full One man then ises and puts away his things and so on until all are comfortably seated.

EXTRACT FROM BATTALION ORDERS NO 71 DATED MARCH 30

MOVE. The Battalion will move from the 96 to the 97th Brigade on the 31st inst Battalion will parade in full marching order ready to march at 0900 (It trams procured time for parading will be altered verbal instructions being issued.

O. C. Coys, Q. Master Messing Officer Pioneer Sergt N.C.O. in charge of drums, P.M.C. Officer's and Sergts Messes Transport Officer and Med Officer are held responsible that all buildings store rooms etc, are left clean when parading, this will include passages etc adjoining rooms.

TRANSPORT.

Transport Officer will arrange for Transport to proceed by road ready to move at 0900 hrs.

BAGGAGE.

All Officers baggage kits etc Quartermasters stores and other stores will be ready to load at 0800 hrs.

MESSING STORES.

Messing stores will be ready to load up as soon as possible after breakfast meal has been issued, and utensils cleaned and packed up.

HEADQUARTERS COMPANY.

Lt Bradley will collect Headquarters Company and will proceed with them as a seperate unit during move

BARRACK STORES.

A, Complete list of all Barrack store handed over to the 1/5th Border Regt with receipts attached will be forwarded to the Adjutant by the Quartermaster as soon as completed.

Original.

SECRET.

WAR DIARY OF

51st Bn. MANCHESTER REGT

APRIL 1919.

Army Form C. 2118.

WAR DIARY
or
INTELLIGENCE SUMMARY.
(Erase heading not required.)

51st MANCHESTER REGT.

Instructions regarding War Diaries and Intelligence Summaries are contained in F.S. Regs., Part II. and the Staff Manual respectively. Title pages will be prepared in manuscript.

Hour, Date, Place	Summary of Events and Information	Remarks and references to Appendices
1/4/19 SEIGBURG MULDORF.	Coy Drill - Handley of Arms under Coy Comdrs. Football in afternoon. 2/Capt. LATURVEY, LT E LEES & 2/LT C.H. BRABHAM joined for duty	[A]
2/4/19 "	Drill as for 1st. CAPT C O WALKER, LT S E GWINNELL, 2/LT P M RYAN & 2/LT AITKEN-DAVIES taken on strength.	[A]
3/4/19 BIELMICHSTEN	B Coy moved into the outpost line, making its HQ at BOCKEROTH and taking over posts 4 & 5 at BOCKEROTH & FRECKWINKEL from A Coy. C. Coy moved into STIELDORF and D Coy into RAUSCHERDORF. Battn H.Q. established at BIELMICHSTEN.	[A]
4/4/19 "	A civilian charged with "failing to raise his hat to a British Military Officer" dealt with by the Community Officer - fined 50 marks.	[A]
5/4/19 "	Inspection by Companies in vicinity of billets. Handling of arms to widen Coy Comdrs. Two sentries erected at FRECKWINKEL when troops pass through the outpost line with head of coat in rear.	[A]
6/4/19 "	LT O HAMILTON joined for duty. Church Parade.	[A]

Army Form C. 2118.

WAR DIARY
or
INTELLIGENCE SUMMARY.   51st Manchester Regt
(Erase heading not required.)

Instructions regarding War Diaries and Intelligence Summaries are contained in F.S. Regs., Part II. and the Staff Manual respectively. Title pages will be prepared in manuscript.

Hour, Date, Place	Summary of Events and Information	Remarks and references to Appendices
7/4/19 BIRLINGHOVEN	Training by Coys during morning. Football – Sports in afternoon. Two civilians arrested 5th inst. were charged with (1) "Attempting to get through Outpost line"; (2) "Attempting to bribe sentry". The case against one civilian was dismissed. In the other case the accused was found guilty only on charge No 1, & fined 30 marks. [A] Capt. T. RICE (CF) attached Batt. Training to go for 7th inst. These civilians were charged with "Failing to raise their hats to British Military Officers" & fined 60, 80, & 100 marks were inflicted. [A]	
8/4/19		
9/4/19 " 10/4/19 " 11/4/19 "	Training under Coy Comdrs during morning. Sports in afternoon. 2/Lt A COLLENS DCM reported for duty on 9/4. A – B. Coys training. C – D Coys Route March during morning. Lecture by member of RATA at STIELDORF A – B. Coys training. C – D Coys to HQ Coys in the afternoon. Sports – Boxing & Football in the afternoon. CAPT. MANSEAGA, LT J.W. BRADLEY, 2/LT C HEWITT – 10/R [A] demobilized.	

Army Form C. 2118.

WAR DIARY
or
INTELLIGENCE SUMMARY.
(Erase heading not required.)

Instructions regarding War Diaries and Intelligence Summaries are contained in F. S. Regs., Part II. and the Staff Manual respectively. Title pages will be prepared in manuscript.

Hour, Date, Place	Summary of Events and Information	Remarks and references to Appendices
BISLINGHOVEN		
11/4/19 Cont.	2 x O/R's despatched on reembarkment furlough. [AS]	
2200 hrs 11/4/19	Four shots were fired by A + B Coys at two men that apparently passed along the front of both Coys. These men believed to be Bolsheviks as parties have been reported in Neutral Zone. Specially was seen from houses in FRECKWINKEL + STIGLDORFERHOHN to Neutral Zone, but occupants of houses escaped. [AS]	
12/4/19 "	Training under Coy Comdrs. Sports in afternoon. Party of 10 O/R proceeded in trip on Rhine to COBLENZ, under a Bn. attach. [AS]	
13/4/19 "	Church Parades. Training. Education, + Sports Programme issued for week ending 19th April. Lt W. H. BOMONEY despatched for demobilization. [AS]	See Appendices "A" "B" "C" attached
14/4/19 "	Training. Sports + Education according to Program. [AS] Lt R. G. CROWE reported for duty with the Batt. and posted to B Coy. [AS]	

Army Form C. 2118.

WAR DIARY
or
INTELLIGENCE SUMMARY.
(Erase heading not required.)

Instructions regarding War Diaries and Intelligence Summaries are contained in F.S. Regs., Part II. and the Staff Manual respectively. Title pages will be prepared in manuscript.

Hour, Date, Place	Summary of Events and Information	Remarks and references to Appendices
15/4/19 BIELINGHOVEN	Training, Sports & Education in accordance with program. Lecture at STIELDORF by Lt. Col. HEPTIS on Military Geography. A civilian was given permission to pass through outpost at STIELDORFERHOHN with a load of mangel. On inspection the cart was found to contain flour, grain, potatoes & bread. Concealed under the mangels, & the civilian was arrested.	[A.1]
16/4/19 "	Training to program. — The Army Comdr. Genl. Sir HERBERT C.O. PLUMER G.C.B. G.C.M.G., G.C.V.O., A.D.C., Corps Comdr. Lt. Gen. Sir T.L.N. MORLAND K.C.B., K.C.M.G., D.S.O. — the Divnl Comdr. Maj. Gen. Sir H.S. JEUDWINE K.C.B. visited the Battn. front line Coys met the Commanding Officer. 2/Lt FOSTER dispatched for demobilization.	[A.2]
17/4/19 "	Training to program.	[A.3]
18/4/19 "	GOOD FRIDAY. Church Parades. 4% dispatched Concentration Camp for demobilization	[A.3]
19/4/19 "	Training & Sports in accordance with program.	[A.3]
20/4/19 "	Church Parade.	[A.3]

Next program of Training, Education & Sports issued for week ending 26/4/19. 1 Appx. See Appendix 'D' D.E.F.

(73989) W4141—463. 400,000. 9/14. H.&J.Ltd. Forms/C.2118/10.

Army Form C. 2118.

WAR DIARY
or
INTELLIGENCE SUMMARY.
(Erase heading not required.)

Instructions regarding War Diaries and Intelligence Summaries are contained in F.S. Regs., Part II. and the Staff Manual respectively. Title pages will be prepared in manuscript.

Hour, Date, Place	Summary of Events and Information	Remarks and references to Appendices
21/4/19 BIRLINGHOVEN	The Army Comdr. Gen¹ SIR W. ROBERTSON, G.C.B, K.C.V.O, D.S.O, A.D.C. visited the Bn¹ton front line Coys. Training re to programs.	(a)
22/4/19 "	Meeting in of Outposts with Saland unit from ferme completed. Civilian arrested 15/4/19 fined 500 marks by the Civil Administrators Court. Training Reduction. - Spoke to programs issued Transport inspection by A.D.V.S.	(a) (a) (a) (a)
23/4/19 "	Training re to programs.	(a)
24/4/19 } 25/4/19 } " 26/4/19 }	CAPT F. WOLFENDEN - L¹ T.O.M.FFOULKS. despatched for demobilization. Church Parades 11°/R despatched for demobilization Training programs for weekendays	(a) (a)
27/4/19 "	Owing to meetings of civilians in neutral territory having been held, at which it is stated a	Appendices "A" "H" "I" (a)

WAR DIARY
or
INTELLIGENCE SUMMARY.

(Erase heading not required.)

Army Form C. 2118.

Hour, Date, Place	Summary of Events and Information	Remarks and references to Appendices
27/4/19 BIRLINGHOVEN	resolution was passed to render all British & French Officers of the Army of Occupation, all Officers have been warned to carry pistols or revolvers at all times, — to avoid being out alone at night. The following is an extract of Bns R.O. on subject:— "In future Officers will carry pistols or revolvers at all times when not in billets in barracks, except when actually playing games. When going to or returning from games Officers will be armed".	[a]
29/4/19	Training. Sports & Education in accordance with programme issued.	
29/4/19		
30/4/19	During the month the hulk of Battn has been fair, 20 O.R. only being transferred to hospital.	[a]
	Strength 52 O/rs 979 O.R.	

P. C. Edgerton. Lt. Col.
Comdg. 5/1st Manchester Regt.

Appendix "A"

51st Bn The Manchester Regiment.

TRAINING PROGRAMME FOR WEEK ENDING APRIL 19th 1919

DATE.	TIME.	NATURE OF TRAINING.	LOCATION TRAINING.
April 14th	0900-1200	At disposal of Coy Commanders for Individual training	Battalion Area
April 15th	0900-1200	At disposal of Coy. Commanders for Individual Training.	Battalion Area.
April 16th	0900-1200	Route March.	
April 17th	0900-1200	At disposal of Coy Commanders for Individual Training.	Battalion Area.
18	0900-1230	Route March.	
April 19th.	0900-1230	Cleaning of Billets, Kit Inspection. Rifle Inspection.	Battalion Area.

11-4-1.
Headquarters.

Lieut Colonel Comdg.,
51st Bn The Manchester Regiment.

51ST IN THE MANCHESTER REGIMENT.

PROGRAMME OF EDUCATIONAL TRAINING FOR W. E. APRIL 19TH 1919.

Coy	Day	Time	Subject	Instructor
C.	Monday	1415-1515	A. Special Subjects. B. Citizenship C. " "	A. Lt Whiteside. B. Sgt Thornton. C. Sgt, " C. Sgt Lambert
	"	1515-1615	A. Special subjects, B. Arithmetic. C. " "	
	Wednesday	0930-1030	A. Special subjects. B. Geography. C. " "	
	"	1030-1130	A. Special subjects B. Arithmetic C. " "	
	Friday.	1415-1515	A. Special subjects B. English History C. " "	
		1515-1615	A Special subjects B. English. C. " "	
D.	Monday	1415-1515	A. Special Subjects B. Citizenship C. " "	A. Sgt Holden B. Lt Mullhollan C. Lt Murray,
		1515-1615	A. Special subjects B. Arithmetic C. " "	
	Wednesday	0930-1030	A. Special subjects B. Geography C. " "	
		1030-1130	A. Special sub, B. Arithmetic C. " "	
	Friday	1415-1515	A. Special sub, B. English History C. " "	
		1515-1615	A. English B. English. C. English.	
A.	Tuesday	1415-1515	A. Special sub, B. Citizenship C. " "	A. Sgt Holden B. Lt Mullhollan C. Lt Murray
		1515-1615	A. Special sub, B. Arithmetic C. " "	
	Thursday	1415-1515	A. Special sub, B English H. C. " "	
		1515-1615	A. Special sub, B " " C English	
	Saturday	0930-1030	A. Special sub, B Geography C. " "	
		1030-1130	A Special sub, B Arithmetic C. " "	
B.	Tuesday	1415-1515	A Special sub, B. Citizenship C. " "	A. Lt Whiteside B. Sgt Thornton C. Sgt Lambert
		1515-1615	A. Special Sub B Arithmetic C " "	
	Thursday	1415-1515	A. Special sub, B English H C " "	
		1515-1615	A. Special sub, B English C " "	
	Saturday	0930-1030	A. Special Sub, B. Geography C " "	
		1030-1130	A. Special sub, B. Arithmetic C " "	

Appendix B.

War Diary — *Appendix C*

SPORTS PROGRAMME FOR WEEK ENDING APRIL 18TH 1919

Date	Units	Coy	Event	Time	Place
14-4-19.	2 Platoons	D. Coy.	Boxing	1800 hrs	Rauchendorf.
15-4-19.	2 "	C "	Association	1430 hrs	Stieldorf.
	2 "	D. "	Running	1430 "	"
	2 "	C "	Boxing	1430 "	"
16-4-19	2 "	A. "	Association	1430 "	"
	2 "	B. "	Running	1430 "	"
17-4-19.	2 "	A. "	Boxing	1430 "	"
	2 "	C. "	Running	1430 "	"
	2 "	D. "	Soccer	1430 "	"
18-4-19	2 "	B "	Soccer	1430 "	"
	2 "	A. "	Running	1430 "	"
	2 "	B "	Boxing	1930 "	"

This cancels previous programme issued as owing to events clashing with Education Programme this had to be readjusted.

Steildorf.

C.M. Hansard,
Sports Officer.

51st THE MANCHESTER REGIMENT.

TRAINING PROGRAMME FOR WEEK ENDING APRIL 26th 1919

DATE.	TIME	NATURE OF TRAINING.	LOCATION TRAINING.
April 21	0900-1200	Sectional training under Coy Commanders.	Battalion Area.
April 22	0900-1200	Sectional Training under Coy Commanders.	Battalion Area.
April 23	0900-1200	Route March.	
April 24	0900-1200	Sectional Training under Coy Commanders.	Battalion Area.
April 25	0900-1200	Sectional Training under Coy Commanders.	Battalion Area.
April 26	0900-1200	Sectional Training under Coy Commanders.	Battalion Area.

51st Bn The Manchester Regiment.

Programe of Educational Training for Week Ending April 26th 1919

CDY.	DAY.	TIME.	SUBJECT.	INSTRUCTOR.
A	Mon.	1415-1515	(a) Special Subjects. (b) Geog.& Gen.Knowledge. (c) do do do	(a) Sgt Holden. (b) Lt.Mulholland (c) Lt.Murray
"	"	1515-1615	(a) Special Subjects. (b) Arithmetic. (c) do	(a) Sgt.Holden. (b) Lt.Murray. (c) Lt.Mulholland.
"	Wed.	0930-1030	(a) Special Subjects. (b) English History (c) do do	(a) Sgt.Holden. (b) Lt.Mulholland (c) do.
"	"	1030-1130	(a) First Aid. (b) do do (c) Arithmetic	(a) Sgt.Thornton. (b) do (c) Lt.Mulholland.
"	Fri.	1415-1515	(a) Citzenship (b) do (c) do	(a) do. (b) do (c) do
"	"	1515-1615	(a) Special Subjects. (b) English (c) do	(a) Sgt Holden. (b) Lt.Mulholland. (c) Lt.Murray.
B	Mon.	1415-1515	(a) Special Subjects (b) Geog.& Gen.Knowledge (c) do do do	(a) Lt.Whiteside. (b) Sgt Thornton. (c) Sgt Lambert.
"	"	1515-1615	(a) Special Subjects. (b) Arithmetic. (c) do	(a) Lt.Whiteside. (b) Sgt Thornton. (c) Sgt Lambert.
"	Wed.	0930-1030	(a) Special Subjects. (b) English History (c) do do	(a) Lt.Whiteside. (b) Lt.Fryer. (c) do
"	"	1030-1130	(a) Special Subjects. (b) First Aid. (c) Arithmetic.	(a) Lt.Whiteside. (b) Sgt Lambert. (c) L/Cpl.Marris.
"	Fri.	1415-1515	(a) Citzenship. (b) do (c) do	(a) Lt.Fryer. (b) do (c) do
"	"	1515-1615	(a) Special Subjects. (b) English. (c) do	(a) Lt.Whiteside. (b) Sgt.Thornton. (c) L/C Marris.
C	Tue.	1415-1515	(a) Special Subject. (b) Geo.& Gen Knowledge. (c) do do do	(a) Lt.Whiteside. (b) Sgt Lambert. (c) Sgt Thornton.
"	"	1515-1615	(a) Special Subjects. (b) Arithmetic. (c) do	(a) Lt.Whiteside. (b) Sgt Thornton. (c) Sgt Lambert.
"	Thur.	1415-1515	(a) Citizenship (b) do (c) do	(a) Lt.Fryer. (b) do (c) do
"	"	1515-1615	(a) First aid (b) do do (c) Arithmetic	(a) Sgt Lambert. (b) do (c) L/C Marris.
"	Sat.	0930-1030	(a) English History (b) do do (c) do do	(a) Lt.Fryer. (b) do (c) do
"	"	1030-1130	(a) Special Subjects. (b) English (c) do	(a) Lt.Whiteside. (b) Sgt Thornton. (c) L/C Marris

EDUCATION TRAINING PROGRAMM

Tue.	1415-1515	(a) Special Subjects.	(a) Sgt Holden.
		(b) Geog.& Gen Knowledge.	(b) Lt. Mulholland.
		(c) do do do	(c) Lt. Murray.
	1515-1615	(a) Special Subjects.	(a) Sgt Holden.
		(b) Arithmetic.	(b) Lt. Murray.
		(c) do	(c) Lt. Mulholland.
Thur.	1415-1515	(a) Citizenship	(a) Lt. Mulholland.
		(b) do	(b) do
		(c) do	(c) do
	1515-1615	(a) Special Subjects.	(a) Sgt Holden.
		(b) First Aid.	(b) Sgt Thornton.
		(c) Arithmetic.	(c) Lt. Mulholland.
Sat.	0930-1030	(a) English History.	(a) do
		(b) do do	(b) do
		(c) do do	(c) do
	1030-1130	(a) Special Subjects.	(a) Sgt Holden.
		(b) English	(b) Lt. Mulholland.
		(c) do	(c) Lt. Murray.

Headquarters,
17-4-19

Signed V. Mulholland Lieut.
Educ. Officer
51st Bn The Manch Regt.

"F"

51stBN THE MANCHESTER REGIMENT.

SPORTS PROGRAMME FOR WEEK ENDING APRIL 26th 1919

DATE	TEAMS	SPORT	TIME	PLACE
21-4-19	No.10 v 11 Platoons	Assoc. Football	14-30	Stieldorf
	No.14 v 13 do	Running	15-30	do
22-4-19	No.2 v 4 do	Assoc. Football	14-30	do
	No.8 v No.7 do	Running	15-30	Bockeroth
	No.13 v 15 do	Boxing	19-30	Rauchendorf
23-4-19	No.9 v Winner of 10&11 Platoons	Assoc Football	14-30	Stieldorf
	No.10 v 12 Platoon	Running	15-30	do
24-4-19	No.2 v 3 do	do	15-30	do
	No.3 v 4 do	Boxing	19-30	do
25-4-19	No.5 v 6 do	Running	15-30	Bockeroth
	No.3 v Winner of No 1&4 Platoons Boxing		19-30	Stieldorf
21/26-4-19	Battalion	Cricket Pratice (if ground available)		

Headquarters

Signed C.M.Hansard Lieut.
Officer I/C Sports.
51st Bn The Manchester Regt.

WAR DIARY
or
INTELLIGENCE SUMMARY.   51 Manchester Regt.
(Erase heading not required.)

Army Form C. 2118.

Hour, Date, Place	Summary of Events and Information	Remarks and references to Appendices
1-5-1919. Billighoven	"C" Company relieved "A" Company taking over 1, 2 & 3 Posts. Relief completed by 12:00 hours. Section training carried on under own Company Comd's. Warrant & Guards to England in force.	
2-5-1919. Billighoven	Creation front thought occupied Territory used by the Re-nunciation examined as an orderly manner. May Day celebrations complete.	
3-5-1919. Billighoven	Section training continued. Letter Deuntary whereas "B" Company taking over 4 & 5 posts. Relief completed by 14:00 hours.	
4-5-1919. Billighoven	Swine Survey arranged for all Companies in the area.	
5-5-1919. Billighoven	Lt.Col. H.F. Walton came. D.S.O. wounded and took over Hdqrs from Major Brown. Foreign D.Rs. Training of Pers under Coy Commanders.	
6-5-1919.	Hqrs saw programme D&o reported troops army in area with Regt Quart-Marshall annual for training.	

Army Form C. 2118.

WAR DIARY
or
INTELLIGENCE SUMMARY.
(Erase heading not required.)

Instructions regarding War Diaries and Intelligence Summaries are contained in F. S. Regs., Part II. and the Staff Manual respectively. Title pages will be prepared in manuscript.

Hour, Date, Place	Summary of Events and Information	Remarks and references to Appendices
7-5-19 to 14-5-1919	Training carried on. Musketry exceptionally heavy. Guards very keen.	
15-5-1919 Billingham	Letters of Company returned — to Malin sent to its Divisional Commander (Major General Sir H. Jeudwine, K.C.B.)	
16-5-1919 17-5-1919 18-5-1919 Billingham	Training carried on as usual. Defence scheme reorganised on 18-5-1919.	
19-5-1919	Report to C in C— Re Command received yesterday was specialist Guards in the 57th Division Force —	
20-5-1919	Diary of Pro Return received for the Special Battalion as they fell. Young	

Army Form C. 2118.

WAR DIARY
or
INTELLIGENCE SUMMARY.
(Erase heading not required.)

Instructions regarding War Diaries and Intelligence Summaries are contained in F. S. Regs., Part II. and the Staff Manual respectively. Title pages will be prepared in manuscript.

Hour, Date, Place	Summary of Events and Information	Remarks and references to Appendices
20/5/1919	[illegible handwritten entries]	
22-5-1919		
23-5-1919		
24-5-1919		
25-5-1919		
26-5-1919		
27-5-1919		
28-5-1919		
29-5-1919		
30-5-1919		
31-5-1919		

51st BN THE MANCHESTER REGIMENT.

TRAINING PROGRAMME FOR WEEK ENDING MAY 3rd 1919

DATE.	TIME.	NATURE OF TRAINING.	LOCATION TRAINING.
Apr. 28	0900-1200	Sectional Training under Coy Commanders.	Battalion Area.
Apr. 29	0900-1200	Sectional Training under Coy Commanders.	Battalion Area.
Apr. 30	0900-1200	Route March.	
May 1	0900-1200	Sectional Training under Coy Commanders.	Battalion Area.
May 2	0900-1200	Sectional Training under Coy Commanders	Battalion Area.
May 3	0900-1200	Sectional Training under Coy Commanders.	Battalion Area.

Birlinghoven
24-4-19

Lieut Col. Commanding,
51st Bn The Manchester Regiment.

51st BN THE MANCHESTER REGIMENT.

TRAINING PROGRAMME FOR WEEK ENDING MAY 3rd 1919

DATE.	TIME.	NATURE OF TRAINING.	LOCATION TRAINING.
Apr. 28	0900-1200	Sectional Training under Coy Commanders.	Battalion Area.
Apr. 29	0900-1200	Sectional Training under Coy Commanders.	Battalion Area.
Apr. 30	0900-1200	Route March	
May 1	0900-1200	Sectional Training under Coy Commanders.	Battalion Area.
May 2	0900-1200	Sectional Training under Coy Commanders	Battalion Area.
May 3	0900-1200	Sectional Training under Coy Commanders.	Battalion Area.

Birlinghoven
21-4-19

Lieut Col. Commanding,
51st Bn The Manchester Regiment.

War Diary

"H"

51st BN THE MANCHESTER REGIMENT.

SPORTS PROGRAMME FOR W/E MAY 3rd 1919

DATE.	TEAMS.	SPORT.	TIME.	PLACE.
27-4-19	51 Mancs. v 53 Mancs.	Soccer.	1430	Menden,
28-4-19	No. 1 Pltn. v No.4	Running.	1530	Stieldorf.
"	" 8 " v " 7	do	1530	do
29-4-19	" 10 " v " 12	do	1530	do
"	" 13 " v " 16	do	1530	do
30-4-19	" 5 " v " 6	do	1530	do
	Winner of 10&12 v " 9	do	1530	do
1-5-19	No. 9 Pltn. v " 11	Soccer (Inter Pltn)	1430	do
2-5-19	Winner of 8&7 Pltn. v winner of 5&6	Running	1530	do
3-5-19	51st Mancs. v 32nd M.G.C. Soccer 51st Mancs. v 13th K.L.R. Rugby.	) Not definite.		

NOTE.

The cricket pitch will be ready on Wednesday & available for practising on, during the evenings or any afternoon when a football match is not being played.

Birlinghoven.
25-4-19

Badge Capt & Adj
Lieut Col Comdg.
51st Bn The Manchester Regiment.

War Diary

51st BN THE MANCHESTER REGIMENT.

PROGRAM OF EDUCATION TRAINING FOR W/E 23rd 1919

COY.	DAY.	TIME	SUBJECT.	INSTRUCTOR.
C	Mon.	1415-1515	a. Special Subject. b. Geo. & Gen Knowledge c. do do	a. Sgt. Holden. b. Lt. Mulholland. c. Lt. Murray.
		1515-1615	a. Special Subject. b. Arithmetic. c. do	a. Sgt. Holden. b. Lt. Murray. c. Lt. Mulholland.
	Wed.	0930-1030	a. Special Subject. b. English History. c. do do	a. Sgt. Holden. b. Lt. Mulholland. c. do
		1030-1130	a. First Aid. b. do do c. Arithmetic	a. Sgt. Thornton. b. do do c. Lt. Mulholland.
	Fri.	1415-1515	a. Citizenship b. do c. do	a. Lt. Mulholland. b. do c. do
		1515-1615	a. Special Subject b. do do c. Arithmetic	a. Sgt. Lambert. b. do c. Lt. Murray.
D. Coy.	Mon.	1415-1515	a. Special Subjects. b. Geography G.K. c. do do	a. Lt. Whiteside. b. Sgt. Thornton. c. Sgt. Lambert
		1515-1615	a. Special Subjects b. Arithmetic c. do	a. Lt. Whiteside. b. Sgt. Thornton. c. " Lambert
	Wed.	0930-1030	a. Special Sub. b. English History c. do do	a. Lt. Whiteside. b. Lt. Fryer. c. do
		1030-1130	a. First Aid b. do do c. Arithmetic	a. Sgt. Lambert. b. " " c. " Thornton.
	Fri.	1415-1515.	a. Citizenship b. " c. "	a. Lt. Fryer. b. " c. "
		1515-1615	a. Special Sub. b. English. c. do	a. Lt. Whiteside b. Sgt. Thornton. c. " Lambert
A.	Tues.	1415-1515	a. Special Sub. b. Geog. G Knowledge c. do do	a. Lt. Whiteside b. Sgt. Thornton. c. " Lambert
		1515-1615	a. Special Sub. b. do do c. Arithmetic.	a. Lt. Whiteside b. Sgt. Thornton. c. " Lambert
	Thursday.	1415-1515	a. Citizenship b. do c. do	a. Lt. Fryer b. do c. do
		1515-1615	a. First Aid b. do do c. Arithmetic	a. Sgt. Lambert b. " " c. Sgt. Thornton
	Saturday	0930-1030	a. English History b. do do c. do do	a. Lt. Fryer b. do c. do
		1030-1130	a. Special Sub. b. English do c. do	a. Lt. Whiteside b. Sgt. Thornton c. do do

continued.

LPL.	DAY.	TIME.	SUBJECTS.	INSTRUCTORS.
B.	Tues.	1415-1515	a Special Sub,	a Sgt Holden,
			b Geog, & G.Knowledge	b Lt Mulholland
			c do do	c Murray
		1515-1615	a Special Sub,	a Sgt Holden
			b Arithmetic	b Lt Murray
			c do	c Lt Mulholland
	Thursday	1415-1515	a Citzenship	a Lt Mulholland
			b do	b do
			c do	c do
		1515-1615	a Special Sub.	a Sgt Holden
			b First Aid,	b Sgt Thornton
			c Arithmetic	c Lt Mulholland
	Saturday	0930-1030	a English History	a Lt Mulholland
			b do do	b do
			c do do	c do
		1030-1130	a Special Sub,	a Sgt Holden
			b English H.	b Lt Mulholland
			c do	c Murray,

BIRLINGHOVEN.

24-4-19.

Lieut: Colonel, Commdg,

51st Bn, The Manchester Regiment.

51st BN THE MANCHESTER REGIMENT.

SPORTS PROGRAMME FOR W/E MAY 3rd 1919

DATE.	TEAMS.	SPORT.	TIME.	PLACE.
27-4-19	51 Mancs. v 53 Mancs.	Soccer.	1430	Menden.
28-4-19	No. 1 Pltn. v No.4	Running.	1530	Stilldorn.
"	" 8 " v " 7	do	1530	do
29-4-19	" 10 " v " 12	do	1530	do
"	" 13 " v " 16	do	1530	do
30-4-19	" 5 " v " 6	do	1530	do
	Winner of 10&12 v " 9	do	1540	do
1-5-19	No. 2 Pltn. v " 11	Soccer (Inter Pltn)	1430	do
2-5-19	Winner of 8&7 Pltn. v winner of 5&6	Running	1530	do
3-5-19	51st Mancs. v 52nd M.G.C. Soccer 51st Mancs. v 13th K.L.R. Rugby,	} Not definite.		

NOTE.

The cricket pitch will be ready on Wednesday & available for practis-ing on, during the evenings or any afternoon when a football match is not being played.

Birlinghoven.
25-4-19

Lieut Col Comdg.
51st Bn The Manchester Regiment.

51st BN THE MANCHESTER REGIMENT.

PROGRAMME OF EDUCATION TRAINING FOR W/E May 3rd 1919

COY.	DAY.	TIME	SUBJECT.	INSTRUCTOR.
C	Mon.	1415-1515	a. Special Subject. b. Geo. & Gen Knowledge. c. do do do	a. Sgt. Holden. b. Lt. Mulholland. c. Lt. Murray.
		1515-1615	a Special Subject. b. Arithmetic. c. do	a. Sgt. Holden. b. Lt. Murray. c. Lt. Mulholland.
	Wed.	0930-1030	a Special Subject. b. English History. c. do do	a Sgt Holden. b Lt. Mulholland. c. do.
		1030-1130	a First Aid. b. do do c Arithmetic	a. Sgt Thornton. b. do do c. Lt Mulholland.
	Fri.	1415-1515	a Citizenship b do c do	a Lt. Mulholland. b do c do
		1515-1615	a Special Subject b do do c Arithmetic	a Sgt Lambert. b do do c Lt. Murray.
D. Coy.	Mon.	1415-1515	a Special Subjects. b Geography G.K. c do do	a Lt Whiteside. b Sgt Thornton. c Sgt Lambert.
		1515-1615	a Special Subjects b Arithmetic c do	a Lt Whiteside. b Sgt Thornton. c " Lambert
	Wed.	0930-1030	a Special Sub. b English History c do do	a Lt Whiteside. b Lt Fryer. c do
		1030-1130	a First Aid b do do c Arithmetic	a Sgt Lambert. b " " c " Thornton.
	Fri.	1415-1515	a Citizenship b " c "	a Lt Fryer. b " c "
		1515-1615	a Special Sub. b English. c do	a Lt Whiteside b Sgt Thornton. c " Lambert
A.	Tues.	1415-1515	a Special Sub. b Geog. G Knowledge c do do	a Lt Whiteside b Sgt Thornton. c " Lambert
		1515-1615	a Special Sub. b do do c Arithmetic.	a Lt Whiteside b Sgt Thornton. c " Lambert
	Thursday.	1415-1515	a Citizenship b do c do	a Lt Fryer b do c do
		1515-1615	a First Aid b do do c Arithmetic	a Sgt Lambert b " " c Sgt Thornton
	Saturday	0930-1030	a English History b do do c do do	a Lt Fryer b do c do
		1030-1130	a Special Sub. b English do c do	a Lt Whiteside b Sgt Thornton c do do

continued.

LRT.	DAY.	TIME.	SUBJECTS.	INSTRUCTORS.
B.	Tues.	1415-1515	a Special Sub, b Geog, & G.Knowledge c do do	a Sgt Holden, b Lt Mulholland c Murray
		1515-1615	a Special Sub, b Arithmetic c do	a Sgt Holden b Lt Murray c Lt Mulholland
	Thursday	1415-1515	a Citizenship b do c do	a Lt Mulholland b do c do
		1515-1615	a Special Sub. b First Aid, c Arithmetic	a Sgt Holden b Sgt Thornton c Lt Mulholland
	Saturday	0930-1030	a English History b do do c do do	a Lt Mulholland b do c do
		1030-1130	a Special Sub, b English H. c do	a Sgt Holden b Lt Mulholland c Murray.

BIRLINGHOVEN.

24-4-19.

Lieutt Colonel, Commdg,

51st Bn, The Manchester Regiment.

51ST. BN. THE MANCHESTER REGIMENT.
SPORTS PROGRAMME FOR W.E. MAY 10TH 1919.

DATE.	TEAMS.	SPORT.	TIME.	PLACE.
May 3rd.	51st Manch. V 38nd M.G.C.	Soccer	1530	Sportsplatz Cologne and Bonn.
" 4th.	No 2 V No 9	Inter Btn. Soccer	1430	Stiffdorf.
" 5th.	" 13 " 4	Soccer.	1430	"
" 6th	" 5 " 6	Running	1530	"
" 7th	" 10 " 5	Boxing.	1830	"
" 8th	" 3 " 13	"	1830	"
" 9th	" 7 " 9	Soccer.	1430	"
" 10th	" or }	51st Manch. V 53 Manch. Soccer	1130	1500
" 11th	" " }			Stiffdorf or London.

(Sgd) G.S.Thwaites,
Sports Officer.

51ST. BN. THE MANCHESTER REGIMENT.
PROGRAMME OF TRAINING FOR W.E. MAY 10TH 1919.

DATE.	TIME.	NATURE OF TRAINING.	LOCATION OF TRAINING.
May 5th	0900-1200	Platoon training under Coy Commdr.	Battalion Area.
May 6th	0900-1200	Platoon training under Coy Commdr.	Battalion Area.
May 7th	0900-1200	Route March.	
May 8th	0900-1200	Platoon training, under Coy Commdr.	Battalion Area.
May 9th	0900-1200	Platoon training under Coy Commdr.	Battalion Area.
May 10th	0900-1200	Platoon training under Coy Commdr.	Battalion Area.

Headquarters.

Lieut. Colonel, Commdg,
51st Bn The Manchester Regiment.

51st Lt THE MANCHESTER REGIMENT.

PROGRAMME OF EDUCATIONAL TRAINING FOR WEEK ENDING MAY 16th 1919

COY.	DAY.	TIME.	SUBJECT.	INSTRUCTOR.
A	Mon.	1415-1515	Special Subject.	Sgt Holden.
			Geo. & Gen. Knowledge.	Lt. Mulholland.
			do do do	Lt. Murray.
	"	1515-1615	Special Subject.	Sgt. Holden.
			Arithmetic.	Lt. Murray.
			do	Lt. Mulholland.
	Wed.	0930-1030	Special Subject.	Sgt Holden.
			English History.	Lt. Mulholland.
			do do	do
	"	1030-1130	First Aid.	Sgt Lambert.
			do do	do
			Arithmetic.	Lt. Mulholland.
	Fri.	1415-1515	Citizenship	Lt. Mulholland.
			do	do
	"	1515-1615	Special Subject.	Sgt Holden.
			English	Lt. Mulholland.
			English.	Lt. Murray.
B	Mon.	1415-1515	Special Subject.	Lt. Whiteside.
			Geo. & Gen Knowledge.	Sgt. Thornton.
			do do do	" Lambert.
		1515-1615	Special Subject.	Lt Whiteside.
			Arithmetic.	Sgt Thornton.
			do	" Lambert.
	Wed.	0930-1030	Special Subject.	Lt Whiteside.
			English History.	" Fryer.
	"	1030-1130	do do	do
			First Aid.	Sgt Thornton.
			do do	do
			Arithmetic.	Sgt Lambert.
	Fri.	1415-1515	Citizenship	Lt. Fryer
			do	do
			do	do
		1515-1615	Special Subjects.	Lt. Whiteside.
			English.	Sgt Thornton.
			do	do
C.	Tues.	1415-1515	Special Sub.	Lt Whiteside
			Geog. & Gen Knowl.	Sgt Thornton.
			do do	" Lambert
		1515-1615	Special Sub.	Lt Whiteside
			Arithmetic	Sgt Lambert
			do	" Thornton
	Thurs.	1415-1515	Citizenship	Lt Fryer
			do	do
			do	do
		1515-1615	First Aid.	Sgt Lambert
			do	" "
			Arithmetic	" Thornton.
	Saty.	0930-1030	English History	Lt Fryer
			do do	do
			do do	do
		1030-1130	Special Sub.	Lt Whiteside
			English	Sgt Thornton
			do	do

EDUCATION PROGRAMME CONTINUED FOR W.E. MAY 10TH;

COY.	DAY.	TIME.	SUBJECTS.	INSTRUCTOR
D.	Tues.	1415-1515	Special Sub, Geog, & Gen. Knowl.	Sgt. Holden. Lt Mulholland.
			do do	Lt Murray.
		1515-1615	Special Sub	Sgt Holden
			Arithmetic,	Lt Murray.
			do	Lt. Mulholland.
	Thurs.	1415-1515	Citizenship	Lt Mulholland.
			do	do
			do	do
		1515-1615	First Aid.	Sgt Thornton.
			do	do
			Arithmetic	Lt Mulholland.
	Saty.	0930-1030	English History	Lt Mulholland.
			do do	do
			do do	do
		1030-1130	Special Sub,	Sgt Holden
			English History	Lt Mulholland
			do do	Lt Murray.

(Sgd) T.Mulholland. Lieut.

30-4-19.

51st BN THE MANCHESTER REGIMENT

SPORTS PROGRAMME FOR WEEK ENDING MAY 18th 1919.

DATE.	TEAMS.	S/CAT.	TIME.	PLACE.
12-5-19	5th Platoon v 6th Pltn.	Running.	1530	Stieldorf.
13-5-19	9th Pltn. v 13th Pltn.	Running.	1530	Stieldorf.
14-5-19	A.Coy v B.Coy.	Soccer.	1530	Stieldorf.
15-5-19				
16-5-19	3rd Pltn. V 13th Pltn.	Boxing (Semi-Final)	1930	Stieldorf.
17-5-19	Hd.Qrs Coy. v B.Coy Kings L.Regt	Soccer.	1430	Stieldorf.
18-5-19	51st Manch. v 53rd Manch.	Soccer.	1430	Neider Plois

8-5-19

(Sgd.) G.S.Thwaites, Lieut.
Bn.Sports Officer.

51st BN THE MANCHESTER REGIMENT.

PROGRAMME OF EDUCATIONAL TRAINING FOR WEEK ENDING MAY 17th 1919.

COY.	DATE.	TIME.	SUBJECT.	INSTRUCTOR.
A	Mon.	1415-1515	Special Subject.	Sgt Holden.
			Geo & Gen Knowledge	Lt. Mulholland.
			do do do	Lt. Murray.
		1515-1615	Special Subject.	Sgt Holden.
			Arithmetic.	Lt. Murray.
			do	Lt. Mulholland.
	Wed.	0930-1030	English History.	do
			do do	do
			do do	do
		1030-1130	First Aid.	Sgt Lambert.
			do	do
			Arithmetic.	Lt. Mulholland.
	Fri.	1415-1515	Citizenship	do
			do	do
			do	do
		1515-1615	Special Subject	Sgt Holden.
			English.	Lt. Mulholland.
			do	Lt. Murray.
B	Mon.	1415-1515	Special Subject.	Lt. Whiteside.
			Geo.& Gen.Knowledge	Sgt Thornton.
			do do do	" Lambert
		1515-1615	Special Subject.	Lt. Whiteside.
			Arithmetic.	Sgt Lambert.
			do	" Thornton.
	Wed.	0930-1030	English History	Lt. Fryer.
			do	do
			do	do
		1030-1130	First Aid.	Sgt Thornton.
			do	do
			Arithmetic.	Lt. Whiteside.
	Fri.	1415-1515	Citizenship	Lt. Fryer.
			do	do
			do	do
		1515-1615	Special Subject	Lt. Whiteside.
			English History.	Sgt Thornton.
			do	do
C	Tue.	1415-1515	Special Subject.	Lt Whiteside.
			Geo & Gen.Know.	Sgt Thornton
			do do do	" Lambert
		1515-1615	Special Subject	Lt Whiteside.
			Arithmetic.	Sgt Thornton.
			do	Sgt Lambert
	Thur.	1415-1515	Citizenship	Lt Fryer.
			do	do
			do	do
		1515-1615	First Aid.	Sgt Lambert.
			do	do
			Arithmetic.	Lt Whiteside.
	Sat	0930-1030	English History	Lt Fryer
			do do	do
			do do	do
		1030-1130	Special Subject.	Lt Whiteside.
			English	Sgt Thornton.
			do	do

51st BN THE MANCHESTER REGIMENT.

D	Tue.	1415-1515	Special Subject.	Sgt Holden.
			Geog. & Gen. Knowl.	Lt. Mulholland.
			do do do	Lt. Murray.
		1515-1615	Special Subject.	Sgt Holden.
			Arithmetic.	Lt. Murray.
			do	Lt. Mulholland.
	Thr.	1415-1515	Citizenship	do
			do	do
			do	do
		1515-1615	First Aid.	Sgt Thornton.
			do do	do
			Arithmetic.	Sgt Holden.
	Sat.	0930-1030	English History.	Lt. Mulholland.
			do	do
			do	do
		1030-1130	Special Subject.	Sgt Holden.
			English.	Lt. Mulholland.
			do	Lt. Murray.

Birling haven.   (Sgd) W. Mulholland Lieut.,
                                   Bn Education Officer.

51st BN THE MANCHESTER REGIMENT.

TRAINING PROGRAMME FOR WEEK ENDING MAY 24th 1919

DATE.	TIME.	NATURE OF TRAINING.	LOCATION TRAINING.
19-5-19	0900-1200	Coy Training under Coy Commanders.	Battalion Area.
20-5-19	0900-1200	Coy Training under Coy Commanders.	Battalion Area.
21-5-19	0900-1200	Route March.	
22-5-19	0900-1200	Coy Training under Coy Commander	Battalion Area.
23-5-19	0900-1200	Coy Training under Coy Commander.	Battalion Area.
24-5-19	0900-1200	Coy Training under Coy Commander	Battalion Area.

Headquarters.
16-5-19

Lieut Col Comdg.
51st Bn The Manchester Regiment.

51st BN THE MANCHESTER REGIMENT.

SPORTS PROGRAMME FOR WEEK ENDING MAY 24th 1919

DATE.	TEAMS.	SPORT.	TIME.	PLACE.
18-5-19	51st Manos. V 53rd Manos.	Soccer.	1430	Neider Plois.
19-5-19	7th Pltn. V 14th Pltn. x(Pltn Knock-Out)	Soccer.	1800	Stieldorf.
20-5-19	2nd Pltn. V 4th Pltn.	Soccer.	1800	do
21-5-19	"C"Coy V "D"Coy (Friendly)	do	1500	do.
22-5-19	9th Pltn V 11th Pltn. x(Pltn.Knock Out)	Soccer.	1800	do
23-5-19	4th Pltn. V 13th Pltn. x(Pltn.Knock Out)	Soccer.	1800	do
24-5-19	"A"Coy V "B" Coy (Friendly)	Soccer.	1500	do

X This competition was commenced at Bonn, and it has now been decided to continue same.

Headquarters.
16-5-19

(Sgnd.) G.S. Thwaites, Lieut.
Bn Sports Officer.

51st BN THE MANCHESTER REGIMENT

PROGRAMME OF EDUCATIONAL TRAINING FOR WEEK ENDING MAY 24th 1919.

COY	DAY.	TIME.	SUBJECT.	INSTRUCTOR.
A	Mon.	1415-1515	Special Subject.	Sgt Holden.
			Geo. & Gen. Know.	Lt. Mulholland.
			do, do, do.	Lt. Murray.
		1515-1615	Special Subject.	Sgt Holden.
			Arithmetic.	Lt. Murray.
			do	Lt. Mulholland.
	Wed.	0930-1030	English History.	do.
			do	do.
			do	do
		1030-1130	First Aid.	Sgt Lambert.
			do	do.
	Fri.	1415-1515	Arithmetic.	Lt. Mulholland.
			Citizenship.	do
			do	do
			do	do
		1515-1615	Special Subject.	Sgt Holden.
			English.	Lt Mulholland.
			do	Lt. Murray.
B	Mon.	1415-1515	Special Subject.	Lt. Whiteside.
			Geo. & Gen. Know.	Sgt Thornton.
			do do do	Sgt Lambert
		1515-1615	Special Subject.	Lt. Whiteside.
			Arithmetic.	Sgt Lambert
	Wed.	0930-1030	do	Sgt Thornton.
			English History.	Lt. Fryer.
			do	do
			do	do
		1030-1130	First Aid.	Sgt Thornton.
			do	do
		1415-1515	Arithmetic.	Lt. Whiteside.
			Citizenship.	Lt. Fryer.
			do	do
			do	do
		1515-1615	Special Subject.	Lt. Whiteside.
			English.	Sgt Thornton.
			do	do
C	Tue.	1415-1515	Special Subject.	Lt. Whiteside.
			Geo. & Gen Know.	Sgt Thornton.
			do do do	Sgt Lambert.
		1515-1615	Special Subject.	Lt. Whiteside.
			Arithmetic,	Sgt Thornton.
			do	Sgt Lambert.
	Thur.	1415-1515	Citizenship.	Lt. Fryer.
			do	do
			do	do.
		1515-1615	First Aid	Sgt Lambert.
			do	do
	Sat.	0930-1030	Arithmetic.	Lt. Whiteside.
			English History.	Lt Fryer.
			do	do
			do	do
		1030-1130	Special Subject.	Lt Whiteside.
			English.	Sgt Thornton.
			do	do

EDUCATION PROGRAMME CONTD.

COY.	DATE.	TIME.	SUBJECT	INSTRUCTOR.
D	Tue.	1415-1515	Special Subject.	Sgt Holden.
			Geo., & Gen Know.	Lt Mulholland.
			do do do	Lt Murray.
		1515-1615	Special Subject.	Sgt Holden.
			Arithmetic.	Lt Murray.
			do	Lt. Mulholland.
	Thur.	1415-1515	Citizenship.	Lt Mulholland.
			do	do
			do	do
		1515-1615	First Aid.	Sgt Thornton.
			do	do.
	Sat.	0930-1030	Arithmetic.	Sgt Holden.
			English History.	Lt Mulholland.
			do do	do
		1030-1130	Special Sbject.	Sgt Holden.
			English.	Lt Mulholland.
			do	Lt Murray.

Headquarters.
15-5-1.

(Sgnd) W Mulholland Lieut
Battalion Education Officer.

51st Bn THE MANCHESTER REGIMENT.

SPORTS PROGRAMME FOR WEEK ENDING MAY 31st 1919

DATE.	TEAMS.	SPORT.	TIME	PLACE.
24-5-19	B Coy	Coy Athletic Sports		Rauchendorf.
25-5-19	Battalion.	Preliminary for Calais Sports 100 yds, 440 yds & 1 Mile	1730 hrs.	Birlinghoven
26-5-19	No 7 Pltn V /4th Pltn.	Soccer.	1800	Stieldorf.
27-5-19	4th Pltn. V 16th Pltn	do	1430	do
28-5-19	Hd Qrs Coy V D.Coy	do	1800	do.
29-5-19	2nd Pltn. V 8th Pltn.	do	1800	do
30-5-19	9th Pltn. V 4th Pltn.	do	1430	do
31-5-19	B Coy V C Coy	do	1500	do
1-6-19	51st Manos. V 52nd Manos	do	1500	Damroich.

Headquarters.
(Sgnd) G.S.Thwaitles. Lieut.
Bn Sports Office.

51st Bn The Manchester Regiment.

TRAINING PROGRAMME FOR WEEK ENDING MAY 31st 1919

DATE.	NATURE OF TRAINING.	LOCATION.
26-5-19	Pltn Training under Coy Commanders.	Battalion Area.
27-5-19	Pltn Training under Coy Commanders.	Battalion Area.
29-5-19	Pltn Training under Coy Commanders.	Battalion Area.
30-5-19	Pltn Traing under Coy Commanders.	Battalion Area.
31-5-19	Pltn Training under Coy Commander.	Battalion Area.
28-5-19	Route March.	

Headquarters.
23-5-19

Lieut Col Commanding.
51st Bn The Manchester Regiment.

51ST BN THE MANCHESTER REGIMENT.

OF EDUCATIONAL TRAINING FOR WEEK ENDING MAY 31st 1919

	COY.	TIME.	SUBJECT.	INSTRUCTOR.
Mon.	A	1145-1245	First Aid.	Sgt Lambert.
Tue.	"	1700-1800	English History.	Lt Mulholland.
"	"	1800-1900	English.	Sgt Firth.
Thur.	"	1145-1245	Geography.	Sgt Holden.
Fri.	"	1700-1800	Citizenship.	Lt Mulholland.
"	"	1800-1900	Arithmetic.	Sgt Holden.
Mon.	B.	1145-1245	First Aid.	Sgt Thornton.
Tue.	"	1700-1800	English History.	Lt Fryer.
"	"	1800-1900	English.	Sgts. Thornton & Smith.
Thur.	"	1145-1245	Geography.	do do do
Fri.	"	1700-1800	Citizenship.	Lt Fryer.
"	"	1800-1900.	Arithmetic.	Sgt Lambert.
Mon.	C	1700-1800	English History.	Lt Fryer.
"	"	1800-1900	English.	Sgt Thornton.
Thur.	"	1700-1800	Citizenship.	Lt Fryer.
"	"	1800-1900	First Aid.	Sgt Lambert.
Mon	D	1600-1700	English History.	Lt Mulholland.
"	"	1700-1800	English.	Sgt Holden.
Thur.	"	1600-1700	Citizenship.	Lt Mulholland.
"	"	1700-1800	First Aid.	Sgt Thornton.
Wednesday.		0900-1200	Instructors Preparation.	
Saturday		0900-1200	Instructors Conference.	

Headquarters.   (Sgd.) V.Mulholland, Lieut.
                       Bn Education Officer.

JUNE 1919.

WAR DIARY
or
INTELLIGENCE SUMMARY. 51st Manchester Regiment
(Erase heading not required.)

Army Form C. 2118.

Hour, Date, Place	Summary of Events and Information	Remarks and references to Appendices
1/6/19 BIRLINGHOVEN	Church Parade. Football in afternoon. Orders have been received for Military Training to be limited to 3 hrs per day; 1½ educational hr. (including lectures) + all afternoons are kept free for sport and amusements.	[A] [A] [A]
2/6/19	Coy Training. Demonstration by a platoon of D Coy.	[A]
3/6/19	Field Sports in afternoon.	[A]
4/6/19	Field Training [A?] Coy Training. Musketry on Range. Sports etc in afternoon.	[A]
	Route March. Operation Orders No. 1, 2 + 3 attached relating to action to be taken if final Peace Terms are not accepted by enemy.	[A] Appendices "A.B.C."
5/6/19	Training under arms only to cut lectures on "War Savings Certificates".	[A]
6/6/19		[A]
7/6/19	Coy Training. All Coys had extra hrs + pistol in morning for escaped enemy prisoners. Parades	

2

Army Form C. 2118.

WAR DIARY
or
INTELLIGENCE SUMMARY.
(Erase heading not required.)

Instructions regarding War Diaries and Intelligence Summaries are contained in F.S. Regs., Part II. and the Staff Manual respectively. Title pages will be prepared in manuscript.

Hour, Date, Place	Summary of Events and Information	Remarks and references to Appendices
6/6/19 BRUNCHON	had been appointed by D.A.P.M. a few days before + accepted upon from his charge on that afternoon	
7/6/19 "	of 6th the is believed to have received the Neutral Zone.	(A)
8/6/19 "	Church Parade.	
9/6/19 "	Whitsun Holiday. No Parade. Sports + Games during day	(A)
10/6/19 "	Training by these Coys. B Coy on Range Cricket Match in afternoon	(A) (B)
11/6/19 "	Route March	
12/6/19 } " 13/6/19 }	Training + Education, one Coy on range each day. Education at least hour in morning Sports in afternoons	(A) (B)
14/6/19 "	Battn Parade. Sports in afternoon. Programe of Training "Education", + Sports for week ending 21/6/19. Inter Batten Sports with 52nd Bn Kings Own	(A) (C)
15/6/19	Church Parade. Sports as above continued. Weather in a.m. Preparing for 52nd Kings Own R of 1 front Brigade attending 'C' a. attached put	Appendices @ "D" "E" + "F" Appendices "C" a

Army Form C. 2118.

WAR DIARY
or
INTELLIGENCE SUMMARY.
(Erase heading not required.)

Instructions regarding War Diaries and Intelligence Summaries are contained in F.S. Regs., Part II. and the Staff Manual respectively. Title pages will be prepared in manuscript.

Hour, Date, Place	Summary of Events and Information	Remarks and references to Appendices
16/6/19 BIRLINGHOVEN	Orders & Instrs to prepare	
17/6/19	Notification received that Y¹ day will be 20th June. Details given in Appendices "D", "E", "F".	
18/6/19	Y¹ day has been postponed, but troops are to be considered to have moved tomorrow.	
19/6/19 DAMBROICH	A Coy moved from STIELDORF to RAUSCHENDORF and HQ from BIRLINGHOVEN to DAMBROICH. Afternoon was completed. Coys were as follows:— front line Coys C & D at OLINGHOVEN and BUCKEROTH respectively. A & B Coys at RAUSCHENDORF, & Hqrs at DAMBROICH.	JN.
20/6/19 "	Bn standing by awaiting orders	
21/6/19 "	Same disposition. C.O¹ passed Dambroich.	JN.

Army Form C. 2118.

WAR DIARY
or
INTELLIGENCE SUMMARY.
(Erase heading not required.)

Instructions regarding War Diaries and Intelligence Summaries are contained in F.S. Regs., Part II. and the Staff Manual respectively. Title pages will be prepared in manuscript.

Hour, Date, Place	Summary of Events and Information	Remarks and references to Appendices
22/6/19 Dambrai	Church Parade. Rested short v. party of 52nd Kings at Dambrai. CSR	
23/6/19 "	General Holiday. Batln Rds shoot. CSR	
24/6/19 "	Rain. Coy lectures in billets. H.Q. Coy on range afternoon. CSR	
25/6/19 "	C.O's Parade. A Coy move from Rumbeke to STIELDORF. Afternoon Inspection now done prior to examination except HQ. Coy in Dambrai. Mounted Div. Sports. CSR	
26/6/19	to Birlinghoven. Received orders to move out A + 3 days. A Coy not yet notified. Coy training. H.Q. on range. Rifle Pool shoot. 50 men B.Coy out - C.R. on detached to mend 3 day working party.	
27/6/19	Coy training. D" on range. N-o4 Operations re A Coy Rublishof. CSR	

(73969) W4141-463. 400,000. 9/14. H.&J.Ltd. Forms/C. 2118/10.

Army Form C. 2118.

WAR DIARY
or
INTELLIGENCE SUMMARY.
(Erase heading not required.)

Instructions regarding War Diaries and Intelligence Summaries are contained in F.S. Regs., Part II. and the Staff Manual respectively. Title pages will be prepared in manuscript.

Hour, Date, Place	Summary of Events and Information	Remarks and references to Appendices
28/6/19	One received that PEACE SIGNED at 16.00 hours. "A" day stated to be Thursday 30/6/19. Educational programme approved by G.O.C.	
29/6/19	Church Parades. Battn. Book shot in afternoon. Ambrose Range.	
30/6/19	B.H.Q. moved at 09.00 hours to BIRLINGHOVEN. See Attendue H.	

A. Walton Lt Col
Commanding
51st Manchester Regt

51st BATTALION MANCHESTER REGT.

OPERATION ORDER NO.1.

"J" - 2 DAYS.

The following action will be taken on "J" - 2 days:-

1. All ammunition limbers will loaded up - Lewis Gun Waggons will be loaded with guns, grenades, flares, etc., as laid down in Divisional Circular No.7.

2. Baggage wagons will report to Q.M. Store.

3. Iron Rations will be drawn from Refilling Point.

4. Normal system of supply will be instituted. Supply wagons will deliver supplies to Units.

5. Ammunition will be brought up to 120 rounds per man. (Indents should be got ready immediately).

6. Surplus kits, blankets, etc., will be collected and stored at Niederpleis.

7. A Guard of 1 N.C.O. and 4 men (B.11's) will be detailed by R.S.M. and will accompany first load to Niederpleis. They will take 3 days supplies of preserved rations. Q.Mr. and all heads of Departments will prepare lists in triplicate of all stuff sent to Dump.

8. Brigade School breaks up - personnel rejoin Companies.

9. Civil Administrator will call up ear marked wagons and horses and send to Companies.

10. Coys. will carry out inspection of Rifles, Kits, feet, equipment, ammunition. The Transport Officer will carry out a complete inspection of all horses and vehicles in addition to inspection of personnel, etc.

11. O.C. "C" Coy. will detail 2 N.C.Os. and 6 men to take over each post at Stieldorferhohn and Freckwinkel. Lieut. Gower, his batman, and Train Corporal remain at Station on duty and will be in charge of post. Category B2s should be detailed who are able to use a rifle.
An Officer of 52nd Manchester Regiment will be in charge of Stieldorferhohn Post.
Rations for Posts will be arranged by Division.

1/6/19.

Capt. & Adjt.,
51st Bn. The Manchester Regiment.

51st BATTALION MANCHESTER REGT.

OPERATION ORDER NO.2.   Sheet 2 L
    Ref.Map 1:100,000.

"J" - 1 DAY.

Information.

1. (a) In case the Germans do not sign the Peace Terms, they will be given 72 hours to reconsider after which a general advance will be made on a day which will be known as "J" day.

(b) The Eastern Division will lead moving along the undermentioned roads followed by Lancashire Division.

    1. Hennef Wissen, Siegen;   - 1st King's Bde.
    2. Hennef Walbrol;   - 3rd Manchester Bde.
    3. Siegburg Neustadt;   - 2nd Lancs. Bde.

(c) The American Troops on right will move forward with FRAMKENBURG as their objective, the VI Corps on the left advance towards SOAST. The two last named are not on the reference map; FRAMKENBURG being 43 miles East of OLPE, and SOAST 12 miles North East of ANSBERG.

(d) The ultimate objective of Eastern Division is the area FREUDENBURG - SEIGEN - KIRCHMUNDEN - SCHONHOLTEN - ATTEMDORN - OLPE; and that of the Lancashire Division is the area WISSEN - WALLMENROTH - FREUDENBURG - (exclusive) - OLPE (exclusive) WEGERINGHSN - MEINERZHGN - MARIENHEIDE (exclusive) - MUCH (exclusive ROSBACH (exclusive).

2. The Brigade Group will be concentrated as follows:-

    51st Mans. - RAUCHENDORF - DAMROICH - ROTT.

3. **INTENTION**
    Letter "C" and "D" Coys. will move to ROTT. "A" Coy. will move to RAUCHENDORF. Battalion Hd. Qrs., Transport Section, Bde Light T.M. Battery to DAMROICH.

DRESS.
    Fighting Order. Packs carried on farm waggon Lewis Gun Limber and Cookers will go with their Coys.
On arrival at their Coy Area one runner from each Coy will report at Bn. Hd. Qrs. Signal Officer will connect up with all Coys.

    It is anticipated that orders will be received at about 7 a.m. to concentrate by 0900 hours so that all arrangements must be completed on "J" - 2 days.

            Burgt.
            Capt. & Adjt.,
        51st Bn. The Manchester Regiment.

51st BATTALION MANCHESTER REGT.

OPERATION ORDER NO.3.

"J" DAY.   Ref. 1:100,000. 2 L.

INFORMATION.

1.   On "J" day - which the Americans describe as "D" day, the 2nd. American Division will advance by road SELTERS - HOHN - HERBORN, Divisional Headquarters being established at HOHN on "J" day.

        On "J" day a French Cavalry Division of 3,000 sabres starting from the area PUDERBACH - ROSBACH - HAIGEN, 12 miles S.E. of SIEGEN.

        On "J" day the Eastern Division will move its 1st Brigade Group by lorry along the HENNEF - SIEGEN Road; its 3rd Brigade Group along the MUCH Road and a force, known as Colonel KINNEAR'S Column, along the WALDBROL Road. Its 2nd Brigade Group moves by train.
        Divisional Headquarters, Eastern Division move to SCHONENBERG on the WALDBROL Road.
        Low flying aeroplanes will accompany the 1st Brigade Group, Eastern Division in order to report progress and assist in overcoming local resistance.

2.   The Lancashire Division will move in support to the Eastern Division, along the following roads:-

        1st Brigade Group.   HENNEF - SIEGEN.

        3rd Brigade Group &)   HENNEF - WALDBROL.
        Div. H.Q. Group.   )

        2nd Brigade Group.   SIEGBURG - NEUSTADT.

        The object is to secure control of the Railways and in denying same to the enemy so it will be essential to ensure not only as much railway stock as possible shall be captured, but also the German Railway personnel shall be prevented from leaving their posts. Although most of this work will devolve on the Eastern Division, troops of the Lancashire Division may have to assist.

        The 3rd Manchester Brigade will move in accordance with the attached march table on "J" day. March tables for subsequent days will be issued later.

        The march will be carried out as a tactical exercise.

        The Advance Guard commanded by Lt.-Colonel KELLY, D.S.O., 52nd Manchester Regt. will consist of the under mentioned troops:-

        52nd Manchester Regt.
        1   Section R.E.
        1   Section T.M.B.
        1   Section M.G.Bn.
affiliated troops will report to O.C. Advance Guard at A minus 2 hours on "J" day.

        Brigade Group will march in 3's. the distances to be observed on march will be those laid down under type "B" (see notes on March discipline recently issued by G.H.Q.)

3.
BILLETING PARTY.
        A billeting party of one N.C.O. per Coy. including H.Q. will to Staff Captain at 52nd Manchester H.Q. Reinforcement a time to be notified. Civil Mayors etc.
accompany

OPERATION ORDER NO.3 (CONTINUED).

4.
TRANSPORT.

Echelon A as under will move with Battalion.

4 Lewis Gun Limbers (each in rear of its own Coy.)
In rear of Battalion -
4 Cookers,
2 Water Carts,
4 S.A.A. Limbers,
2 Tool Limbers,
1 Maltese Cart,
3 Pack Animals in the above order.

Echelon B: Remainder of transport will move under orders of Brigade Transport Officer.

5.
DRESS.

Fighting Order, packs on farm wagons. Unexpired portion of days ration plus one Iron ration.
Time for parade and order of march will be notified later.

Capt. & Adjt.,
51st Bn. The Manchester Regiment.

51st Bn Manchester Regiment.

PROPOSED PROGRAMME OF TRAINING FOR WEEK ENDING JUNE, 21st 1919

COY.	TIME.	NATURE OF TRAINING.	PLACE.
A Mon.	0645–	Roll Call & Read Orders.	Stieldorf.
	0800–1800	Musketry.	Damroich.
B "	0645–0745	Arms & Saluting Drill.	Rauchendorf.
	0845–1100	Pltn Exercise (Ball)	Quarry, Freckwinkle.
C, "	0645–0745	Anti-Gas.	Olinghoven.
	0845–1100	Pltn Drill, P.T. & B.F.	do
D "	0645–0745	Musketry Drills.	Pltn Areas.
	0845–1100	No. 16 Pltn Attack with Ball Remainder Pltn Drill Map Reading & Scouting.	
A Tue	0645–0745	Anti-Gas.	Stieldorf.
	0845–1100	P.T. Gas, L.G. & Grenade Firing.	Freckwinkle.
B, "	0645–	Roll Call & Read Orders.	Rauchendorf.
	0800–1800	Musketry Range.	Damroich.
C "	0645–0745	March Discipline.	Olinghoven.
	0845–1100	30 x Range, Lewis Gunning. Grenade Firing.	do Quarry Freckwinkle.
D, "	0645–0745	Musketry Drills.	Pltn Areas
	0845–1100	No. 13 Pltn in attack (Ball) Remainder Lewis Funning & Grenade Training.	Freckwinkle & Duforo
Battalion,	0730–Onwards (Wednesday)	Route March (By Coys)	
A Thur.	0645–0745	Lewis Gunning-Arms Drill.	Stieldorf.
	0845–1100	L. Gunning Bombing, Musketry on Minature Range.	do.
B "	0645–0745	Arms Drill & Saluting Drill	Rauchendorf.
	0845–1100	L.G. Shooting, Tactical Exercise. Rifle Shooting, Fire Discipline & Bombing.	Nr. Oberschuren. Quarry Free.
C "	0645–	Roll Call & Read Orders.	Olinghoven.
	0800–1800	Musketry- Range.	Damroich
D "	0645–0745	Musketry Drill.	Pltn Areas.
	0845–1100	No. 14 Pltn in attack (Ball) No. 15 Pltn in attack (do) Remainder Pltn Drill & Musketry.	Bockeroth. Freckwinkle. do
A Fri.	0645–0730	Pltn Drill & Saluting.	Stieldorf.
	0845–1100	L.G. on Minature Range, P.T., B.F. & Gas.	do
B "	0645–0730	Fire Discipline & Fire Control.	Rauchendorf.
	0845–1100	As for Thursday.	
C "	0645–0730	Arms Drill.	Olinghoven.
	0845–1100	Pltn Exercise. (Ball)	Quarry Freckwinkle.
D "	0645–	Roll Call	Pltn Areas.
	0800–1800	Roll Call & Musketry.	Damroich.
A Sat.	0645–0730	Guards Drill.	Stieldorf.
B. "	0645–0730	Anti - Gas.	Rauchendorf.
C "	0645–0730	Musketry Drills.	Olinghoven.
D "	0645–0730	Anti - Gas.	Pltn Areas.
	0845– Onwards	Battalion Ceremonial Drill.	Stieldorf.

NOTE.

Sports & Education as per Programmes.

Headquarters.
13-6-19

Lieut Col, Comdg.
51st Bn, Manchester Regiment.

51st Bn Manchester Regiment,

PROGRAMME OF EDUCATIONAL TRAINING FOR WEEK ENDING JUNE 21st 1919

DAY.	HOURS.	COY.	SUBJECT.	INSTRUCTOR.
Monday.	1130-1230	A	Arithmetic.	Sgts. Steele & Holden
"	1130-1230	B	English.	Sgts. Smith & Wainwright
"	1130-1230	C	First Aid.	Sgt Lambert.
"	1130-1230	D	English History.	Lt Mulholland.
Tuesday.	1130-1230	A	English.	Sgt Smith & Wainwright
"	1130-1230	B	First Aid.	Sgt Thornton.
"	1130-1230	C	English History.	Lt Mulholland.
"	1130-1230	D	Geography.	Sgts. Steele & Holden
Wednesday.	1130-1230	A	First Aid.	Sgt Lambert.
"	1130-1230	B	English History.	Lt Mulholland.
"	1130-1230	C	Geography.	Sgts. Steele & Smith.
"	1130-1230	D	General Knowledge.	Sgt Holden.
Thursday.	1130-1230	A	English History.	Lt Mulholland.
"	1130-1230	B	Geography.	Sgts Smith & Wainwright
"	1130-1230	C	General Knowledge.	Sgt Thornton.
"	1130-1230	D	Arithmetic.	Sgts Steele & Holden
Friday.	1130-1230	A	Geography.	Sgts Wainwright & Holden
"	1130-1230	B	General Knowledge.	Sgt Thornton.
"	1130-1230	C	Arithmetic.	Sgts Lambert & Steele
"	1130-1230	D	English.	Sgts Smith & Wainwright.
Saturday.	1130-1230	A	General Knowledge.	Sgt Holden.
"	1130-1230	B	Arithmetic.	Sgts Lambert & Steele
"	1130-1230	C	English.	Sgts Smith Wainwright.
"	1130-1230	D	First Aid	Sgt Thornton.

Headquarters.
11-6-19

(Sgnd) W. Mulholland Lieut.
Education Officer,

(6 30 17) W7642—M869 25,000 10/16 HWV(P1116) Forms/W3342/1
2924—M2056 100,000 5/17

Army Form W. 3342.
(M.S. 3522/1.)

RETURN OF REGIMENTAL OFFICERS ENTITLED TO TEMPORARY RANK.

Unit _____

Name (Surname first)	Present rank (Substantive or Brevet)	Temporary rank to date from	Nature of appointment taken up and date	(a) Previous holder of appointment, cause and date of relinquishment. (b) Last substantive holder of appointment; cause and date of relinquishment.	*Date of relinquishing temporary rank and reason

NOTE.—Returns to be submitted direct from Divisional H.Q. to M.S. (G.H.Q.)

Date _____

To Military Secretary,
  General Headquarters.

* Required in retrospective cases only.

_____
(Signature)
Officer Commanding unit.

51st Bn MANCHESTER REGIMENT.

SPORTS PROGRAMME FOR WEEK ENDING JUNE 21st 1919

DATE.	COMPANY.	TIME.	PLACE.	NATURE OF SPORT.
16-6-19	No.1 Pltn.V.No.7 Pltn.	1430	Stieldorf.	Cricket (Inter (Pltn Knock-Out)
17-6-19	No.14 Pltn.V.13 Pltn	1430	do	do
18-6-19	No.2 Pltn V.15 Pltn.	1430	do	do
18-6-19	"A" Company.	1830	do	Whist Drive.
19-6-19	51st Manch Regt. V. 52nd Kings L'pool Regt	1500	Birlinghoven.	Cross-Country 3 miles, 440 yds. 100yds, 1 mile.
20-6-19	"A" Coy V. "B" Coy	1430	Stieldorf.	Cricket.(Inter Coy (Knock Out)
21-6-19	No 8 Pltn V. No.3 Pltn	1430	do	Cricket Inter Pltn Knock Out.
22-6-19	"D" Coy V. Hd.Qrs Coy	1430	do	Cricket Inter Coy.

Cricket
Net practice every afternoon at Stieldorf. An Inter Coy & Inter Pltm Knock Out League commences on 16-6-19 as avove.

Boxing.
Boxers train 3 times a week under Lt Grennan.

Cross Country.
Runners being trained by Lt Mulholland M.C.

-----#-------

Headquarters.
2-6-19

(Sgd) Lt G.A.Thwaits.
Battalion Sports Officer.

Army Form O. 1810
All Arms.

Unit **51st. Bn. Manchester Regiment.**

DAILY ORDERS. PART II. No. 2. Reg.

N.B.—The Sub. No. of Order and Subject are to be shown in cols. 1 and 2, thus :—1. Courts Martial.

Station **G.H.Q. 3rd. Echelon.** Date **31.3.19.**

ORDERLY ROOM
No.
4 APR 1919
MANCHESTER REGT.

Regimental No., Rank and Name.	Sqdn., Batty. or Co.	Particulars of Casualties, etc., and Date.
1. STRENGTH. INCREASE.		
41562 Pte. Warburton. W.	"C"	posted from 2nd. Bn. Manchester Regiment and taken on strength with effect from 18.3.19. Posted to "C" Coy.
2. ERRATUM.		
		Reference Part II Order No. 2 sub-para. 1. Col. 2. dated 24.3.19 Delete 52149 Pte. Fox. W.

3. STRENGTH OF BATTALION 31.3.19.

OFFICERS.	W.Os,	SERGTS.	CORPLS.	L/CPLS.	PRVTES.	TOTAL.
49	7	52	49	42	893	1092

L R Chapman

Captain for,
Officer i/c Infantry Section No. 6.
G.H.Q., B.E.F.

Officer Commanding or Adjutant.

BOXING AT RAUSCHENDORF

SATURDAY JUNE 14TH. 1919 1630 HRS.

WEIGHTS.   8 Stone and under.
                8 Stone to 8 St. 8 lbs.
                8 St. 8 lbs. to 9 St. 6 lbs.
                9 St. 6 lbs. to 10 St. 4 lbs.
                10 St. 4 lbs. to 11 St. 6 lbs.

REFEREE.   LIEUT. BROWN. 3RD. MANCHESTER BRIGADE SCHOOL.

JUDGE.   LIEUT. G.C.P. GRENNAN
                51st MANCHESTERS.

JUDGE.   LT. COL. C.E. ALBIN. D.S.O.
                Commanding, 52nd KINGS.

TIME-KEEPER.   LIEUT. O. HAMILTON.
                51ST. MANCHESTERS.

M.C.   LIEUT. J.E. PEARSON.
                51ST. MANCHESTERS.

                -3-3-3-3-3-3-3-3-3-3-3-3-3-3-3-

SCORING.   2 POINTS FOR WINNER.
                1 POINT FOR LOSER.

MUSKETRY. On the RANGE at DAYROLOI.

SUNDAY JUNE 15TH. 1919. 1030 HRS.

TEAMS OF SIX.

1. APPLICATION at 200x. SIX Rounds
    lying, as in Practice 1 Part II
    (Addendum No. 4.)

2. RAPID   at 200x. 10 Rounds in Magazine.
              Time limit - 1 Minute. No limit
              to number of Rounds fired.

3. SNAP SHOOTING. As in Practice 19, Part III.
              Lying in open. (Addendum No. 4.)

              -3-3-3-3-3-3-3-3-3-3-3-3-3-3-3-

NO PRIZES.   2 POINTS TO WINNING TEAM IN EACH EVENT
              TO COUNT IN AGGREGATE FOR THE WHOLE
              COMPETITION. REGULATION SCORING.

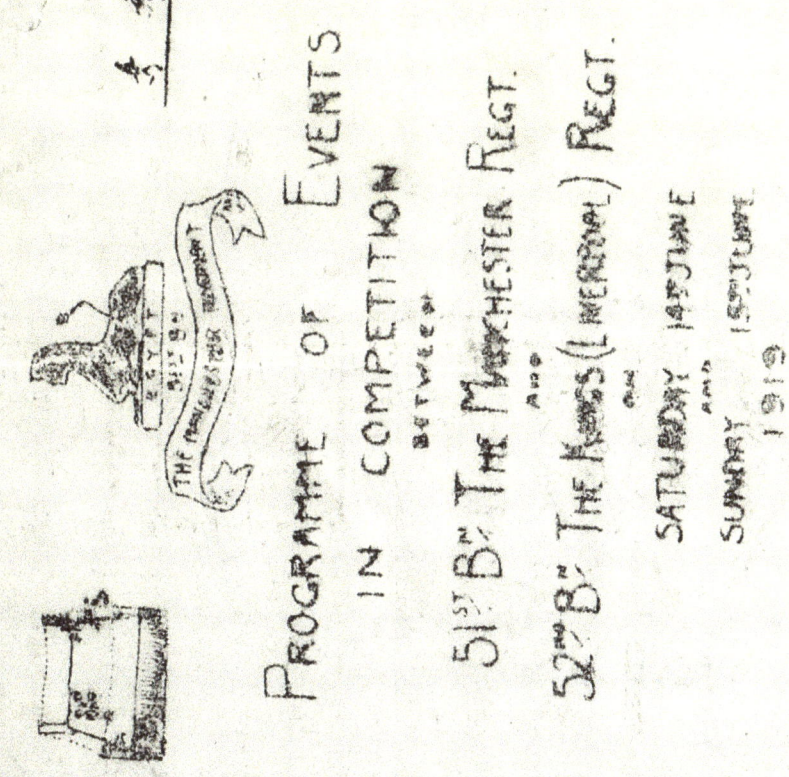

Programme of Events
in competition between
51st Bn The Manchester Regt.
and
52nd Bn The Kings (Liverpool) Regt.

SATURDAY 14th JUNE
and
SUNDAY 15th JUNE
1919

BOXING AT RAUSCHENDORF.

MUSKETRY AT DAMBROICH RANGE.

ATHLETICS AT BIRLINGHOVEN.

ATHLETIC SPORTS at BIRLINGHOVEN.

SUNDAY. JUNE 15TH. 1919. 1700 HRS.

a. 100 yds.   1st_____ 2nd_____
b. Long Jump.   1st_____ 2nd_____
c. 440 yds.   1st_____ 2nd_____
d. Bomb-Throwing. 1st_____ 2nd_____
e. 220 yds.   1st_____ 2nd_____
f. One Mile.   1st_____ 2nd_____

TEAMS OF TWO TO REPRESENT EACH BATTALION.

REFEREE.   LT.COL.H.F.WATSON.CMG.DSO.
              Commanding, 51st. Manchesters.

JUDGES.   MAJOR M.WOOD.MC. 51ST. MANCHESTERS.
              LIEUT. J.R.PENSWICK.   do
              CAPT. W.FOSS.MC. 52ND. KINGS.
              LIEUT. PURCHASE.   do

TIME-KEEPER. CAPT. C.D.WALKER. 51ST. MANCHESTERS.

STARTER.   LIEUT. O.HAMILTON. BRIGADE SCHOOL.

CROSS COUNTRY AT BIRLINGHOVEN. TEAMS OF 10 (NOT MORE
THAN TWO OFFICERS IN EACH TEAM).
DISTANCE - 3 MILES.

-:-:-:-:-:-:-:-:-:-:-:-:-:-:-:-:-:-

XXXIXMAYXBXMAXJXSXMXXXXXXXXXXXXXXXXXXXXXXXXXX

THREE CHEERS FOR THE WINNERS.   HIP-HIP-------

as/a/

PROGRAMME OF EDUCATION FOR WEEK ENDING   G
                                    /6th July./

DAY.	TIME.	COY.	SUBJECT.	INSTRUCTOR.
Mon.	1130 - 1230	A.	Arithmetic.	Sgt. Holden.
			"C" Group. English.	Sgt. Firth.
		B.	English.	Sgt. Wainwright.
			"C" Group. English.	Sgt. Taylor.
		C.	First Aid.	Sgt. Lambert.
			"C" Group. English.	Pte. Paterson.
		D.	English History.	Sgt. Smith.
			"C" Group English.	Lieut. Murray; Pte. Clarke
	1430 - 1630		Book-keeping.	Sgt. Smith.
			Mechanics.	Sgt. Taylor.
Tue.	1130 - 1230	A.	English.	Sgt. Wainwright.
			"C" Arithmetic.	Sgt. Firth.
		B.	First Aid.	Sgt. Thornton.
			"C" Arithmetic.	Sgt. Taylor.
		C.	English History.	Sgt. Smith.
			"C" Arithmetic.	Pte. Paterson.
		D.	Geography.	Sgt. Steele.
			"C" Arithmetic.	Lt. Murray; Pte. Clarke
	1430 - 1530		French.	Sgt. Lambert.
	1530 - 1630		Shorthand. (Elemty)	Sgt. Holden.
Wed.	1130 - 1230	A.	First Aid.	Sgt. Lambert.
			"C" English.	Sgt. Firth.
		B.	English History	Sgt. Smith.
			"C" English.	Sgt. Taylor.
		C.	Geography.	Sgt. Steele.
			"C" English.	Pte. Paterson.
		D.	General Knowledge.	Sgt. Holden.
			"C" English.	Lt. Murray; Pte. Clarke
Thu.	1130 - 1230	A.	English History.	Sgt. Smith.
			"C" Arithmetic.	Sgt. Firth.
		B.	Geography.	Sgt. Wainwright.
			"C" Arithmetic.	Sgt. Taylor.
		C.	General Knowledge.	Sgt. Thornton.
			"C" Arithmetic.	Pte. Paterson.
		D.	Arithmetic.	Sgt. Holden.
			"C" Arithmetic.	Lt. Murray; Pte. Clarke
	1430 - 1630		Book-keeping.	Sgt. Smith.
			Mechanics.	Sgt. Taylor.
Fri.	1130 - 1230	A.	Geography.	Sgt. Wainwright.
			"C" English.	Sgt. Firth.
		B.	General Knowledge.	Sgt. Thornton.
			"C" English.	Sgt. Taylor.
		C.	Arithmetic.	Sgt. Steele.
			"C" English.	Pte. Paterson.
		D.	English.	Lt. Whiteside.
			"C" English.	Lt. Murray; Pte. Clarke
	1430 - 1530		French.	Sgt. Lambert.
	1530 - 1630		Shorthand. (Elemty)	Sgt. Holden.
Sat.	1130 - 1230.	A.	General Knowledge.	Sgt. Holden.
			"C" General Knowledge	Sgt. Firth.
		B.	Arithmetic.	Sgt. Lambert.
			"C" General Knowledge	Sgt. Taylor.
		C.	English.	Lt. Whiteside.
			"C" Gen. Knowledge.	Pte. Paterson.
		D.	First Aid.	Sgt. Thornton.
			"C" Gen. Knowledge.	Lt. Murray.

Education Office.   (Sgd) Dennis Whiteside, Lt.
26/6/18.   Education Officer,
                                        51st Bn. Manchester Regt.

51st BN. THE MANCHESTER REGIMENT.

OPERATION ORDER No. 4.

Reference Sheet S.L. Germany 1:100,000.

INFORMATION.
(1) In the event of Peace Terms being signed without any advance taking place, orders may be expected for the Battalion to move into its normal area and from there to the Menden Area.

INTENTION.
(2)
(a) Battalion Headquarters on "A" Day will move from DAMBROICH to BIRLINGHOVEN; Transport Section to ZECHE PLATO; and will be clear of DAMBROICH by 0950 hours. Details will appear in Bn. Orders.

(b) The 51st Manchesters on "B" Day will move from present area to MENDEN and MEINDORF areas.

ORDERS TO TROOPS.
(3) (a) Hour of start   - 1500 hours.
    (b) Starting point   - Road junction just N.E. of the second N in BIRLINGHOVEN.
    (c) Order of March   - "A" Coy, Bn. Headquarters, "B", "C" and "D" Coys. Transport Section. Machine Gun Limbers and Cookers will follow in rear of their respective Companies.

DETAILS AND ADMINISTRATIVE ORDERS.
(4) (a) Dress   - Full Marching Order, Steel Helmets.
    (b) S.A.A.   - As for training.
    (c) Halts.   - Clock hour halts.
    (d) Reveille.   - 0645 hours.
    (e) Breakfast. - 0745 hours.
    (f) Dinner.   - Dinners will be cooked in kitchens and men will be fed in canteens. O.C. Coys will arrange a suitable place to have dinners in Coy. area. Cookers will then be cleaned and filled with water for tea, between 1200 hours and 1300 hours.
    (g) Tea.   - Hot water will be arranged for so as to be ready to make tea on arrival at MENDEN and MEINDORF. The Master Cook will arrange for hot water to be got ready in conjunction with one or more Coys for Headquarters Coy, and Transport Section.
    (h)   - On arrival in area the R.S.M. will arrange to collect the S.A.A. into a central dump under charge of the Bn. Quarter Guard.
    Reports.   - To Head of Battalion.

27/6/19.

Capt. & Adjt.
51st Bn. The Manchester Regt.

WAR DIARY
or
INTELLIGENCE SUMMARY.
(Erase heading not required.)

Army Form C. 2118.

ORDERLY RO...
No 91980.
1 AUG 1919
...CHESTER REG...

July 1

Instructions regarding War Diaries and Intelligence Summaries are contained in F. S. Regs., Part II. and the Staff Manual respectively. Title pages will be prepared in manuscript.

Place	Date	Hour	Summary of Events and Information	Remarks and references to Appendices
Babyhousen	1/7/19		In accordance with Op. Order 4 (Appen H) June diary, Battn moved to Menden at 1300 hours; 53 transport look over Babyhousen area. On arrival Battn location:- BHQ, B, C & D Coys:- MENDEN A Coy V MEINDORF.	
Menden	2/7/19		Range working Party reported. Bn E Battn.	
"	3/7/19		General Holiday - Races.	
"	4/7/19		All Coys working to complete range. Coy training & rifle bn exercises. Include Inspection A.Q B&D Coy. Competition Platoon.	
"	5/7/19		A & D Coys working on range. Competition Platoon exercises in Training Hook & Educational programme for weekending 13/7/19	A S&T A B E&T B E&T C
"	6/7/19		Indoor Inspection A&C Coys attended. C of E Parade - Chaplain absent. O/Venstock Place. Lied 5 men to rehearsed Bn in Paris. Victory march.	
"	7/7/19		Final Inspection Platoon Test. D Coy winner. C in C	

WAR DIARY or INTELLIGENCE SUMMARY

Army Form C. 2118.

July

Place	Date	Hour	Summary of Events and Information	Remarks and references to Appendices
MENDEN	7/7/19		Btn. (less Palenken) visited Bellaton. HQ A+D Coy Baths and indoor musketry instruction same parade. Frank training programme "Phase D".	2
	8/7/19		Coy training. A+D on range, working parties.	
	9/7/19		Coy training. C O's parade.	
	10/7/19		Coy training.	
	11/7/19		Coy training. Inspected N.G.G.R.M.L. Guard.	
	12/7/19		C O's parade. Training Education & Sport Programme for week ending 19/7/19. Appendices E, F, & G respectively.	E F G
	13/7/19		Church Parades. Lord Raglan met CAMBRAI.	
	14/7/19		Army Education exam. 2nd class. HQ A+B Baths.	
	15/7/19		3rd Class Army Education Exam. C+D Baths.	
	16/7/19		Battalion photograph taken. Won Inter Competition Swimming.	
	17/7/19		Coy training. D Coy on range.	
	18/7/19		Coy training. Plumbing Inspection. I Corps Transport first place. Baths Concert Officer.	K K

WAR DIARY
or
INTELLIGENCE SUMMARY.
(Erase heading not required.)

Army Form C. 2118.

July 3

Place	Date	Hour	Summary of Events and Information	Remarks and references to Appendices
MENDEN	19/7/19		General Holiday - new celebration. Training, Education & Sports Programmes for week ending 26/7/19. Appendices	"A" Appendices "J"
	20/7/19		Church Parades. Cricket: Officers v Rest of Battn. Officers Victory.	
			Pet.	
	21/7/19		Training as per programme.	
	22/7/19		Bde Rifle Sports } Supplementer "L"	"L"
	23/7/19		" " "	
	24/7/19			
	25/7/19		Bde Sports.	
	26/7/19		" " Training, Education & Sports Programme for week ending 2nd Aug 1919, Appendices M N & O respectively. Bde Transport Competition. Cup GIVEN by Medical Inspection. 52 men to hospital	M N O
	27/7/19		Church Parades. Major Berlin Command was Lt Col Osborn on leave.	

Army Form C. 2118.

WAR DIARY
or
INTELLIGENCE SUMMARY.
(Erase heading not required.)

July

Place	Date	Hour	Summary of Events and Information	Remarks and references to Appendices
MENDEN	28/7/19		Training as per programme	
	29/7/19		"C" Coy on Range GMC. "D" Coy inoculation	
			" " " " Brigade Platoon Efficiency Competition	
			Best platoon 52nd bn ordered to compete in Brigade Platoon Efficiency Competition	
	30/7/19		"B" Coy on range. Brigade Platoon Efficiency Competition - 53rd bn Sports Birkenhagen ??	
	31/7/19		Medical Inspection. "C" & "D" Coy Range GMC. "B" Route March. Football - Semi Final	
			Brigade Platoon Sports Cup.	

Capt F Lyle M/61 RGR
Commanding 61st Manchester Rgt.

MCurtis B
1/8/19

51st Battn, The Manchester Regiment

BATTALION CONCERT.

PROGRAMME.

OVERTURE.	At the Piano.	Sgt. Boor.
SONG.		R.S.M. Moore.
RECITATION.	From the North Sea.	Pte Gee H.W.
SONG.		Sgt. Greenwood.
SONG.		Lt. Col. Watson H.F.
SONG.	The Millionaire.	Pte Stott.
RECITATION.	At the Dump.	Lt. Fryer.
SONG.	The Trumpeter.	Sgt. Kirkland.
RECITATION.	The Little Yellow God.	Lt. Fox.
SONG.		Capt. Walker.
INTERLUDE.		Pte Dawson.
SONG.		Lt. Col. Watson.
RECITATION.	To Germany.	Pte Gee H.W.
GLEE.	The Officers Glee Party. "A" Coy.	New and Old boys of "A" Company.

51st Bn Manchester Regiment

SPORTS PROGRAMME FOR WEEK ENDING JULY 19th 1919

DATE.	COY.	TIME.	PLACE.	NATURE OF SPORT
14-7-19	"B" Coy v "D" Coy	1430	Menden B Ground	Cricket
15-7-19	Battalion	1430	do A Ground	Hockey Pick up match
16-7-19	H.Q. Coy v.Winners of match between "A" Coy v Winners of C v D (Sunday)	1430	do A Ground	Soccer
17-7-19	Pde School v Battalion	1430	do B do	Cricket
18-7-19	"A"Coy v "B" Coy.	1430	do A do	Soccer
19-7-19	Officers v Kent Battalion	1430	do B do	Cricket
20-7-19	No 11 Pltn v No 12 Pltn		do A do	Soccer

Cross Country Runners. Athletes,and Boxers will train under Lt Grennan Lt Theakto, and Sgt Barley every Monday, Wed and Saturdays morning.

Hockey — All Officers and Men must turn up on Tuesday Pte.No.

51st BN MANCHESTER REGIMENT.

PROGRAMME OF EDUCATIONAL TRAINING FOR WEEK ENDING JUNE 12th 1919

DAY.	TIME.	COY.	SUBJECT.	INSTRUCTOR.
Mon.	1130-1230	"A"	Arithmetic	Sgt Firth
"	1130-1230	"A"	"C" Group English	Lt Murray
"	" "	"B"	English	Lt Whiteside
"	" "	"B"	"C" Group Eng	Sgt Wainwright
"	" "	"C"	First Aid	Sgt Lambert
"	" "	"C"	"C" Group Arithmetic	Holden
"	" "	"D"	English History	Sgt Smith
"	" "	"D"	"C" Group Gen.Kn	Pte Patterson
"	1430-1530	Spe Classes	Bookeeping	Sgt Smith
"	" "	"	Mechanics	" Taylor
Tue.	1130-1230	"A"	English	Sgt Firth
"	" "	"A"	"C" Group Arithmetic	Lt Murray
"	" "	"B"	First Aid	Sgt Lambert
"	" "	"B"	"C" Group Arith	Sgt Holden
"	" "	"C"	English History	Sgt Smith
"	" "	"C"	"C" Group English	Lt Whiteside
"	" "	"D"	Geography	Sgt Taylor
"	" "	"D"	"C" Group Gen Know.	"Wainwright
"	1430-1530	Special Classes	French	Sgt Lambert
"	1530-1630	" "	Shorthand Elem	Sgt Holden
Wed	1130-1230	"A"	First Aid	Sgt Thornton
"	" "	"A"	"C" Group English	Lt Murray
"	" "	"B"	English History	Sgt Smith
"	" "	"B"	"C" Group English	"Wainwright
"	" "	"C"	Geography	Sgt Taylor
"	" "	"C"	"C" Group Arith.	" Holden
"	" "	"D"	Citizenship	Lt Fryer
"	" "	"D"	"C" Group Gen Know	Pte Clarke
Thur	1130-1230	"A"	English History	Sgt Firth
"	" "	"A"	"C" Group Arith.	Lt Murray
"	" "	"B"	Geography	Sgt Taylor
"	" "	"B"	"C" Group Arith.	Pte Patterson
"	" "	"C"	Citizenship	Lt Fryer
"	" "	"C"	"C" Group English	Sgt Wainwright
"	" "	"D"	Arithmetic	Sgt Holden
"	" "	"D"	"C" Group Gen Know	Lt Whiteside
"	Special Classes	1430-1530	Bookeeping	Sgt Smith
"	" "	1430-1530	Mechanics	Sgt Taylor
Fri	1130-1230	"A"	Geography	Sgt Thornton
"	" "	"A"	"C" Group English	Lt Murray
"	" "	"B"	Citizenship	Lt Fryer
"	" "	"B"	"C" Group English	Sgt Wainwright
"	" "	"C"	Arithmetic	Sgt Holden
"	" "	"C"	"C" Group Arithmetic	Pt Patterson
"	" "	"D"	English	Lt Whiteside
"	" "	"D"	"C" Group Gen Know	Pte Clarke
"	1430-1530	Spe Classes	French	Sgt Lambert
"	1530-1630	"	Shorthand Elem	Sgt Holden
Sat	1130-1230	"A"	"C" Group Gen Know	Sgt Thornton
"	" "	"A"	Arithmetic	Sgt Holden
"	" "	"B"	"C" Group Gen Know	"Taylor
"	" "	"C"	English	Lt Whiteside
"	" "	"C"	"C" Group Gen Know	Pte Patterson
"	" "	"D"	First Aid	Sgt Lambert
"	" "	"D"	"C" Group Gen Know	Wainwright

P. Fryer Lieut

51st Bn Manchester Regiment.

SPORTS PROGRAMME FOR WEEK ENDING JULY 13th 1919

DATE.	COY.	TIME.	PLACE	NATURE OF SPORT.
7-7-19	A Coy V B Cy.	1730	Hendon A Ground	Football
7-7-19	Battalion	From 1430 "	B "	Cricket Practice
8-7-19	C Coy V D Cy.	1430 "	A "	Cricket
9-7-19	No 4 V No 9 Pltn	1430 "		Soccer
10-7-19	No 12 V 13 Pltn	1800 "	A	Cross-Country Bde Final
10-7-19	Battalion	From 1430	A	Cricket Practice
11-7-19	C Coy V D Coy	1800 "	A	Football
12-7-19	Bn H.Q.V Brigade Sch.	1430 "	A	Cricket
13-7-19	13th Pltn V 5 Pltn	1930	H.Q. mess Room	Boxing
13-7-19	Winner A V B Vwinner C V D.	1430	Hendon A Ground	Football

"A" Ground is the one near Bde School
"B" "   "   "   "   "   Transport Lines

Tue, Wed, Thur. mornings the runners and Boxers will train under 2/Lt Grennan and Sgt Earley.

Headquarters.   Sgnd G.S.Thwaites
  5-7-19   Lieut

51st Battn, The Manchester Regiment.

51st Battn, The Manchester Regiment.

PROGRAMME OF EDUCATIONAL TRAINING FOR THE WEEK. ENDING. JULY 26/

DAY.	TIME.	COY.	SUBJECT.	INSTRUCTOR.
Monday.	1130-1230	"A"	Arithmetic.	Sgt, Firth.
"	"	"	"C" Group English.	Lt, Murray, & Sgt Thornt
"	"	B.	English.	Lt Whiteside.
"	"	"	"C" Group English.	Sgt, Wainwright.
"	"	C.	First Aid.	" Lambert.
"	"	"	"C" Group Arithmetic.	" Holden.
"	"	D.	English History	" Smith.
"	"	"	"C" Group Gen, Knowledge.	Pte Paterson.
Tuesday.	1130-1230	"A"	English	Sgt, Firth.
"	"	"	"C" Group Arithmetic	Lt, Murray & Sgt Thornt
"	"	B.	First Aid.	Sgt, Lambert.
"	"	"	"C" Group Arithmetic	Sgt Holden.
"	"	C.	English History	" Smith.
"	"	"	"C" Group English.	Lt, Whiteside.
"	"	D.	Geography.	Sgt, Taylor.
"	"	"	"C" Group Gen. Know.	" Wainwright.
Wednesday.	11-30-1230.	"A"	First Aid.	Sgt, Thornton.
"	"	"	"C" Group English.	Lieut, Murray.
"	"	B.	English History.	Sgt, Smith.
"	"	"	"C" Group English.	Sgt Wainwri
"	"	C.	Geography.	Sgt Taylor.
"	"	"	"C" Group Arithmetic	" Holden.
"	"	D.	Citizenship.	Lt, Fryer.
"	"	"	"C" Group Gen, Know.	Sgt, Steele.
Thursday.	1130-1230.	"A"	English History	Sgt, Firth.
"	"	"	"C" Group, Arithmetic.	Lt Murray & Sgt Thornt
"	"	B.	Geography.	Sgt, Taylor.
"	"	"	"C" Group Arithmetic	Pte Paterson.
"	"	C.	Citizenship.	Lt, Fryer.
"	"	"	"C" Group English.	Sgt, Wainwright.
"	"	D.	Arithmetic.	" Holden.
"	"	"	"C" Group Gen, Know.	Lt, Whiteside.
Friday.	1130-1230.	"A"	Geography.	Sgt, Thornton.
"	"	"	"C" Group Arithmetic.	Lt Murray.
"	"	B.	Citizenship.	Lt, Fryer.
"	"	"	"C" Group English.	Sgt, Wainwright.
"	"	C.	Arithmetic	" Holden.
"	"	"	"C" Group Arithmetic.	Pte Paterson.
"	"	D.	English.	Lt, Whiteside.
"	"	"	"C" Group Gen, Know.	Sgt, Steele.
Saturday	1130-1230	"A"	Citizenship	Lt, Fryer.
"	"	"	"C" Group Gen Know.	Sgt, Thornton.
"	"	B.	Arithmetic.	" Holden.
"	"	"	"C" Group. Gen Know.	" Taylor.
"	"	C.	English.	Lt, Whiteside.
"	"	"	"C" Group, Gen, Know.	Sgt Steele.
"	"	D.	First Aid.	" Lambert.
"	"	"	"C" Group Gen, Know.	" Wainwright.

(Sgd)
P. Fryer, Lt,
Education Officer.
51st Bn, Manchester Regiment.

SPORTS PROGRAMME FOR WEEK-ENDING 27-6-1919

SPORTS PROGAMME FOR WEEK ENDING

Date.	Coy.	Time.	Place	Nature of Sport.
21-7-19	Inter-Company.	18.00.hrs.	Mendon.	X.Country -3 1/2 miles- Teams of 10 per Coy. The 20 best men will represent the Bttn in Divisional Competion.
22-7-19	C.Coy.V.53Mans best Coy, or B.Coy,5&6.V,7&8;	14.30.	" A.Gd. " B.Gd.	1st Round Div Comp.Soccer, Cricket.
23-7-19	Brigade School.	14.30	" " " "	Sports.
24-7-19	A&B.V.C&D.	15.00	" " A.Gd	Hockey.
25-7-19	Battalion.		Sports Platz Cologne Road.--Divnal Sports.
26-7-19	"	"	" " " " " "
27-7-19	51st.Bn.V.Bde.School.	14.30.	Mendon	Cricket.

BOXING. 13 Platoon to report every morning at Sports Office to train. Other Boxers as usual on Monday, Wednesday & Saturday mornings.
X.COUNTRY. All runners to report every Monday, Wednesday & Saturday morning

51st Bn Manchester Regiment.

SPORTS PROGRAMME FOR WEEK ENDING AUGUST 3rd 1919.

DATE.	COY.	TIME.	PLACE.	NATURE SPORT
28- -19	A Coy v B Coy.	1430	Menden B Ground	Cricket.
29-7-19	A & B Coys V C & D Coys.	1430	Menden A Ground	Hockey
30-7-19	Offrs V Rest Bn.	1430	Menden A Ground	Soccer.
31-7-19	C Coy V D Coy.	1400	Menden B Ground	Cricket
1-8-19	Battalion	1500	Starting point) D Coy Mess	Marathon Race - Menden to Birlinghove and back.
2-8-19.	12 Platoon V 4 Ptn.	1430	Menden A Ground	Soccer.
3-8-19	Officers v Rest of Battalion.	1430	Menden B Ground	Cricket.

MENDEN,
24/7/19.

(Sgd) G. S. Thwaits, Lt.
Sports Officer,
51st Bn. The Manchester Regiment.

51st Bn. THE MANCHESTER REGIMENT.

Programme of Educational Training for Week Ending 2/8/19.

Day.	Time.	Coy.	Subject.	Instructor.
Mon.	1130-1230	"A"	Citizenship.	Lieut. Fryer.
"	"	"	"C" Group Arithmetic.	" Murray.
"	"	" "B"	Arithmetic	Sgt. Holden
"	"	"	"C" Group Arithmetic	" Wainwright
"	"	" "C"	Geography	" Taylor
"	"	"	"C" Group Arithmetic	Pte. Paterson
"	"	" "D"	English	Lieut. Whiteside
"	"	"	"C" Group Arithmetic	Pte. Clarke
Tues.	1130-1230	"A"	Geography	Sgt. Thornton
"	"	"	"C" Group English	Lieut. Murray.
"	"	" "B"	Citizenship.	" Fryer.
"	"	"	"C" Group English.	Sgt. Wainwright.
"	"	" "C"	Citizenship	Lieut. Fryer.
"	"	"	"C" Group English.	Pte. Paterson.
"	"	" "D"	Citizenship	Lieut. Fryer.
"	"	"	"C" Group English.	Pte. Clarke
Wed.	1130-1230	"A"	English History.	Lieut. Mullholland.
"	"	"	"C" Group General Knowledge.	Sgt. Firth.
"	"	" "B"	Geography.	Sgt. Smith.
"	"	"	"C" Group General Knowledge.	" Wainwright.
"	"	" "C"	English	Lieut. Whiteside.
"	"	"	"C" Group General Knowledge.	Pte. Paterson.
"	"	" "D"	Arithmetic	Sgt. Holden.
"	"	"	"C" Group General Knowledge	Pte. Clarke.
Thu.	1130-1230	"A"	Arithmetic.	Sgt. Thornton
"	"	"	"C" Group English.	" Murray.
"	"	" "B"	Debates.	Sgt. Smith.
"	"	"	"C" Group English.	" Wainwright.
"	"	" "C"	Debates.	Lieut. Fryer.
"	"	"	"C" Group English.	Pte. Paterson.
"	"	" "D"	Debates.	Sgt. Steele
"	"	"	"C" Group English.	Pte. Paterson.
Fri.	1130-1230	"A"	Debates.	Lieut. Mullholland.
"	"	"	"C" Group Arithmetic.	" Murray.
"	"	" "B"	English.	Sgt. Smith.
"	"	"	"C" Group Arithmetic.	" Wainwright.
"	"	" "C"	Arithmetic.	" Holden.
"	"	"	"C" Group Arithmetic.	Pte. Paterson.
"	"	" "D"	Geography.	Sgt. Taylor.
"	"	"	"C" Group Arithmetic.	Pte. Clark.
Sat.	1130-1230	"A"	English.	Sgt. Firth.
"	"	"	"C" Group General Knowledge.	Sgt. Thornton.
"	"	" "B"	English History.	Lieut. Mullholland.
"	"	"	"C" Group General Knowledge.	Sgt. Wainwright.
"	"	" "C"	English History.	Lieut. Mullholland.
"	"	"	"C" Group General Knowledge	Pte. Paterson.
"	"	" "D"	English History	Lieut. Mullholland.
"	"	"	"C" Group General Knowledge.	Pte. Clarke.

<u>NOTE</u>. Citizenship and English History lectures for "B" "C" and "D" Coys. on Tuesday and Saturday will be held in "D" Coy's Messing Centre.

MENDEN,
23/7/19.

(Sgd) W. Mullholland, L..
Education Officer,
51st Bn. The Manchester Regiment.

51st Bn Manchester Regiment.

PROGRAMME OF TRAINING FOR WEEK ENDING JULY 13th 1919

COY.	TIME.	DATE.	TRAINING.	PLACE.
A	630-730	7-6-19	Rouse Parade	Meindorf. Menden
"	900-1100	"	Pn & Extended Order Drill	"
"	1130-1230	"	Education	"
"		"	Adjt Parade	"
B	630-730	"	1 Pltn Insp; 3 Pltn P.T.	"
"	900-1000	"	Musketry	"
"	1000-1100	"	Education	"
"	1130-1230	"	1/2 Hour Arms Drill	"
C	630-730	"	Extended Order Drill & Pn Drill	"
"	900-1100	"	Education	"
"	1130-1230	"	1/2 Hour Pltn Drill under Platoon Commander.	"
D	0630-0730	"	P.T.B.T.& Anti-Gas	"
"	900-1100	"	Education	"
"	1130-1230	"	R.S.M.	Meindorf.
A	630-730	8-7-19	Rouse Parade.	Menden
"	0900-1100	"	P.T.B.T.& Gas	"
"	1130-1230	"	Education	"
"		"	R.S.M.Parade.	"
B	0630-0730	"	L.G.& Grenade Firing	"
"	0900-1100	"	Education R.S.M.	"
"	1130-1230	"	Rouse Parade	"
C	0630-0730	"	P.T.	"
"	0900-1000	"	Lewis Gun & Grenade	"
"	1000-1100	"	Education R.S.M.	"
"	1130-1230	"	Rouse Parade	"
D	0630-0730	"	Sects. under Sect Comdrs Loading.	"
"	0900-1100	"	Education	"
"	1130-1230	"	Pltn Drill under Coy Comdr	Meindorf
A	0630-0730	9-7-19	Adjts Parade	Bn Exer. Ground
"	0900-1000	"	C.O.Parade	do
"	1000-1100	"	L.G.& Grenade Firing	Menden
"		"	Pn Drill under Coy Commander	"
B	0630-0730	"	C.O.Parade	"
"	0900-1000	"	Extensions	"
"	100-1230	"	Education	"
C	630-0730	"	Pltn Drill under Coy Comm.	"
"	0900-1000	"	C.O.Parade	"
"	1000-1100	"	Anti-Gas	"
"	1130-1230	"	Education	"
D	0630-0730	"	Pltn Drill under Coy Comdr	"
"	0900-1000	"	C.O.Parade	"
"	1000-1100	"	Lewis Gunning	"
"	1130-1230	"	Education	"
A	630-730	10-7-19	R.S.M.Parade	Meindorf. Menden
"	0900-1100	"	L.G.Scouting & Patrolling	"
"	1130-1230	"	Education	"
B	0630-0730	"	R.S.M.Parade	"
"	0900-1100	"	L.G.,Tactical Exer.	"
"	1130-1230	"	Education	"
C	0630-0730	"	R.S.M.Parade	"
"	0900-1100	"	Sect. under Sect Comdrs (Loading)	"
"	1130-1230	"	Education	"
D	0630-0730	"	R.S.M.Parade	"
"	0900-1100	"	Pltn in attack	"
"	1130-1230	"	Education	"

B & D Coy Rouse Parade under Adjt

TRAINING PROGRAMME CONTD.

A	0630-0730	11-7-19	Coy Drill under senior Sergt.	
"	0900-1100	"	Pltn In Attack (Blank)	
"	1130-1230	"	Education	
B	0630-0730	"	Coy Drill under Senior Sgt	
"	0900-1100	"	Coy in attack Preliminary	
"	1130-1230	"	Education	
C	0630-0730	"	Coy Drill (under Senior Cpl)	
"	0900-1100	"	Patrolling & Scouting.	(BC Coy
"	1130-1230	"	Education	(Rose Parade
D	0630-0730	"	Coy Drill under senior Sgt	under
"	0900-1100	"	Coy in attack Prelim.	Adjt.
"	1130-1230	"	Education	

A	0630-0730	12-7-19	R.S.M.Parade (Saluting)	Mond
"	0900-1000	"	C.O.Parade	"
"	1000-1100	"	Guard Drill	"
"	1130-1230	"	Education	"
B	0630-0730	"	R.S.M.Parade (Saluting)	"
"	0900-1000	"	C.O Parade	"
"	1000-1100	"	Guard drill	"
"	1130-1230	"	Education	"
C	0630-0730	"	R.S.M.Parade (Saluting)	"
"	0900-1000	"	C.O.Parade	"
"	1000-1100	"	L.G.& Bombing	"
"	1130-1230	"	Education	"
D	0630-0730	"	R.S.M.Parade (Saluting)	"
"	0900-1000	"	C.O.Parade	"
"	1000-1100	"	Guard Drill	"
"	1130-1230	"	Education	"

PROGRAMME.

TUESDAY.

"A" Coy.	0630 - 0730 hrs.	Arms Drill	Meindorf.
" "	0900 - 1100 "	P.T., B.T., & Gas.	"
	1130 - 1230 "	Education.	"
"B" "	0630 - 0730 "	Arms Drill under R.S.M.	Parade Ground.
	0900 - 1100 "	L.Gunning Grenade	Bn. Parade Ground
	1130 - 1230 "	Education.	Coy.Dining Hall.
"C" "	0630 - 0730 "	Arms Drill under RSM.	Bn. Parade Ground.
	0900 - 1100 "	Education.	Coy.Dining Hall.
	1130 - 1230 "	P.T.,L.G. & Grenade.	Bn.Parade Ground.
"D" "	0630 - 0730 "	Arms Drill under RSM.	Bn. Parade Ground.
	0900 - 1100 "	Section Leading.	" " "
	1130 - 1230 "	Education.	Coy. Dining Hall.

WEDNESDAY.

"A" Coy.	0630 - 0730 hrs.	Platoon Drill	Meindorf.
	0900 - 1000 "	C'O's Parade.	Bn.Parade Ground.
	1000 - 1100 "	L.G. & Grenade firing.	" " "
"B" "	0630 - 0730 "	Pn. Drill under Adjt.	" " "
	0900 - 1000 "	C.O's Parade.	" " "
	1000 - 1100 "	Extensions.	" " "
	1130 - 1230 "	Education.	Coy.Dining Hall.
"C" "	0630 - 0730 "	Pn. Drill under Adjt.	Bn.Parade Ground.
	0900 - 1000 "	C.O's Parade.	" " "
	1000 - 1100 "	Anti-Gas.	" " "
	1130 - 1230 "	Education.	Coy.Dining Hall.
"D" "	0630 - 0730 "	Pn.Drill under Adjt.	Bn.Parade Ground.
	0900 - 1000 "	C.O's Parade.	" " "
	1000 - 1100 "	L.Gunning & Grenades.	" " "
	1130 - 1230 "	Education.	Coy.Dining Hall.

THURSDAY.

"A" Coy.	0630 - 0730 hrs.	Coy. Training.	Meindorf.
	0900 - 1100 "	" "	Bn.Parade Ground.
	1130 - 1230 "	Education.	Coy.Dining Hall.
"B" "	0630 - 0730 "	R.S.M's Parade.	Bn.Parade Ground.
	0900 - 1100 "	Coy. Training.	" " "
	1130 - 1230 "	Education.	Coy.Dining Hall.
"C" "	0630 - 0730 "	R.S.M's Parade.	Bn.Parade Ground.
	0900 - 1100 "	Coy. Training.	" " "
	1130 - 1230 "	Education.	Coy. Dining Hall.
"D" "	0630 - 0730 "	R.S.M's Parade.	Bn.Parade Ground.
	0900 - 1100 "	Coy. Training.	" " "
	1130 - 1230 "	Education.	Coy.Dining Hall.

FRIDAY.

Bn.	0630 - 0730 hrs.	Adjt's Parade.	Bn.Parade Ground.
	0900 - 1100 "	Coy. Training.	" " "
	1130 - 1230 "	Education.	Coys Dining Halls

SATURDAY.

Bn.	0630 - 0730 hrs.	Saluting.(R.S.M)	Bn.Parade Ground.
	0900 - 1000 "	C.O's Parade.	" " "
	1130 - 1230 "	Education.	Coys Dining Halls

This programme cancells all issued previously.

MENDEN.
7/7/19.

Capt. & Adjt.,
The Manchester Regt.

1st Bn Manchester Regiment.

PROGRAMME OF TRAINING FOR WEEK ENDING JULY 19th 1919

COY.	TIME.	NATURE OF TRAINING	PLACE	REMARKS.
A	0630-1230	Coy Drill & Musketry Part 2.	Meindorf Range.	
B	0630-0730	Coy Drill under Adjt.	Bn Parade Ground	
"	0900-1100	Coy in attack (Blank)	do	
"	1130-1230	Education		
C		Coy Drill under Adjt. (0630-0730)	Bn Parade Ground	
"	0900-1100	Coy in attack (Blank)	Vicinity Range.	
"	1130-1230	Education		
D	0630-0730	Coy Drill under Adjt.	Bn Parade Ground.	
"	0900-1100	P.T.Musk.L.G. & Grenades		(L.G. & Grenade under
"	1130-1230	Education.		(Sgts Boor & Lingard.)
A	0630-0730	Arms Drill	Meindorf.	
"	0900-1100	Coy in attack (Blank)	do	
"	1130-1230	Education		
B	0630-0730	Arms Drill under R.S.M.	Bn Parade Ground.	
"	1230	Musketry Part 2.	Range.	
C	0630-0730	Arms Drill under R.S.M.	Bn Parade Ground.	
"	0900-1100	P.T.Musk.L.G. & Grenades		(L.G.& Grenades under
"	1130-1230	Education		(Sgt Boor & Lingard)
D	0630-0730	Arms Drill under R.S.M.	Bn Parade Ground	
"	0900-1100	Coy in attack (Blank)	Vicinity Range.	
"	1130-1230	Education		
A	0630-0730	Coy Drill	Meindorf.	
"	0900-1100	P.T.Musk.L.G. & Grenades		(L.G. & Grenade under
"	1130-1230	Education.		(Sgt Boor & Lingard.)
B	0630-0730	Coy Drill under Adjt.	Bn Parade Ground.	
"	0900-1100	Coy in attack (Blank)	Vicinity Range.	
"	1130-1230	Education		
C	0630-0730	Coy Drill under Adjt.	Bn Parade Ground	
"	1230	Musketry Part 2,	Range.	
D	0630-0730	Coy Drill under Adjt.	Bn Parade Ground	
"	0900-1100	Coy in attack (Blank)	Vicinity Range.	
"	1130-1230	Education		
All Coys.	0700-1200	Route March		Route Ref. Germany Sheet S L 1. 400, 000 squared. Starting Point.
A	0630-0730	Arms Drill	Meindorf	
"	0900-1100	Coy in attack	Vicinity Range.	
"	1130-1230	Education		
B		Arms Drill under R.S.M.	Bn Parade Ground.	
"	0900-1100	P.T Musk.L.G. & Grenades		(L.G.& Grenade under
"	1130-1230	Education		(Sgts Boor & Lingard.)
C	0630-0730	Arms Drill under R.S.M.	Bn Parade Ground	
"	0900-1100	Coy in attack	Vicinity Range.	
"	1130-1230	Education		
D	0630-0730	Arms Drill under R.S.M.	Bn Parade Ground.	
"	0900-1230	Musketry Part 2.	Range.	
All Coys.	0630-0730	Saluting.		
	0900-1100	C.O.'s Parade.	Bn Parade Ground.	
	1130-1230	Education.		

NOTES.

Education carried on daily 1130-1230 in Dining Halls.
2 Examination Subjects will probably take place on Mon & Tuesday.
3 Arrangements made with Mr Nicholson to take Panorama Photograph at 0930 Hours Wed.
4 Blank Amn used for Coy Training owing to range being in use all day

51st Bn Manchester Regiment.

PROGRAMME OF EDUCATIONAL TRAINING FOR WEEK ENDING JULY 12th 1919

DAY	TIME	COY	CO	SUBJECT	INSTRUCTOR
Mon	0900-1230	All Coys		Army Certificate Exam	
Tue.	0900-1230	All Coys		Army Certificate Exam.	
Wed	1130-1230	"A"		First Aid	Sgt Thornton.
"	"	"		"C" Group English	Lt Murray & Sgt Firth
"	"	"	"B"	English History	Sgt Smith
"	"	"	"	"C" Gr. English	Sgt Wainwright
"	"	"	"C"	Geography	Sgt Taylor
"	"	"	"C"	"C" Group Arithmetic	Pte Patterson
"	"	"	"D"	Citizenship	Lt Fryer
"	"	"	"	"C" Group Gen Knowledge	Sgt Steele
Thur	1130-1230	"A"		English History	Sgt Firth
"	"	"		"C" Group Arithmetic	Lt Murray & Sgt Thornton
"	"	"	"B"	Geography	Sgt Taylor
"	"	"	"	"C" Group Arithmetic	Pte Patterson
"	"	"	"C"	Citizenship	Lt Fryer
"	"	"	"	"C" Group English	Sgt Wainwright
"	"	"	"D"	Arithmetic	Sgt Holden
"	"	"	"D"	"C" Group Gen Knowledge	Lt Whiteside
Fri.	1130-1230	"A"		Geography	Sgt Thornton
"	"	"		"C" Group English	Lt Murray
"	"	"	"B"	Citizenship	Lt Fryer
"	"	"	"	"C" Group English	Sgt Wainwright
"	"	"	"C"	Arithmetic	Sgt Holden
"	"	"	"	"C" Group Arithmetic	Pte Patterson
"	"	"	"D"	English	Lt Whiteside
"	"	"	"	"C" Group Gen Knowledge	Sgt Steele
Sat	1130-1230	"A"		Citizenship	Lt Fryer
"	"	"		"C" Group Gen Knowledge	Sgt Thornton
"	"	"	"B"	Arithmetic	Sgt Holden
"	"	"	"	"C" Group Gen Knowledge	Sgt Taylor
"	"	"	"C"	English	Lt Whiteside
"	"	"	"	"C" Group Gen Knowledge	Pte Patterson
"	"	"	"D"	First Aid	Sgt Lambert
"	"	"	"	"C" Group Gen Knowledge	Sgt Wainwright

10-7-19

(Sgnd) E.Fryor Lieut.

Bn Education Officer 51st Manch Regt.

51st Bn Manchester Regiment.

PROGRAMME OF TRAINING FOR WEEK ENDING JULY 26th 1919

COY.	TIME.	NATURE OF TRAINING	PLACE.
A	0630-0730	Under Coy Comdr.	Meindorf.
"	0900-1100	Coy in attack.	do
B	0630-1230	Musketry Part 2.	Range.
C	0630-0730	Adjts Parade	Bn Prade Ground
"	0900-1100	Outpost Duty	Menden
D	0630-0730	Adjts Parade.	Bn Parade Ground.
"	0900-1100	P.T.L.G. Grenade & Gas Training.	L.G.& Grenades under Sgts Boor & Lingard
A	0630-0730	Under O.C. Coy,	Meindorf.
"	0900-1100	P.T.,L.G.,& Grenades.	(L.G.& Grenade Training under Sgts Boor & Lingard
B	0630-0730	R.S.Ms. Parade.	Bn Parade Ground
"	0900-1100	Coy in attack.	Menden
C	0630-1230	Musketry Part2.	Range.
D	0630-0730	R.S.Ms Parade	Bn Parade Ground.
"	0900-1100	Outpost Duty.	Menden
A	0630-0730	Under Coy Comdr.	Meindorf.
"	0900-1100	Coy in defence.	do
B	0630-0730	Adjts Parade.	Bn Parade Ground.
"	0900-1100	Coy in defence.	Menden.
C	0630-0730	Adjts Parade,	Bn Parade Ground.
"	0900-1100	Outpost Duty	Vicinity Range.
D	0630-1230	Musketry Part 2.	Range.

All Coys. 0700-1230 Bn Route March ending in attack.
Starting Point. where track joins
Road just W. of the O. in Obermenden
(All available men are to Square A.33.94. Route notified later
attend Educ Parade

"A"	0630-1300	Musketry G.M.C.	Range.
B.	1300-1800	" "	Range;
C.	0630-0730	R.S.M. Parade.	
	0900-1100	Company as a rear Guard.	Menden.
D.	0630-0730	R.S.M Parade.	
	0900-1100	Company in Defence.	Menden.

Battalion, 0630-0730 Adjutant's Parade.
" 0900-1100 Commanding Officer's Parade.

NOTES.

Education each day 1130-1230. hours.
Wednesdays and Saturday afternoons will be kept clear of
Parades, and administrative duties, 25% of the Company sent for leave
from 1400-2300hrs.
Blank ammunition used for training. Range in use all day.

Lieut, Colonel, Commanding
51st, Btn, The Manchester Regiment.

51st BN. THE MANCHESTER REGIMENT.

PROGRAMME OF TRAINING FOR WEEK ENDING AUGUST 2nd, 1919.

Coy.	Time.	Nature of Training.	Place.
		MONDAY.	
A.	0600-1300	Musketry.	Range.
"	1300-1800	Musketry.	Range.
B.	0630-0730	Adjutant's Parade.	Battalion Parade Gr
C.	0900-1100	Advanced Guard.	Vicinity of Range.
"	0630-0730	Adjutant's Parade.	Battalion Parade
D.	0900-1100	Company in Attack.	" "
		TUESDAY.	
A.	0630-0730	Under O.C. Company.	Meindorf.
"	0900-1100	P.T., L.G., & Grenades.	Menden. *B Coy Inoculation*
B.	0630-0730	R.S.M's Parade.	"
"	0900-1100	Outpost Duties.	"
C.	0600-1300	Musketry.	Range.
D.	1300-1800	"	"
		WEDNESDAY.	
A.	1300-1800	Musketry.	Range. *A Coy - Eng training*
B.	0600-1300	"	"
C.	0630-0730	Adjutant's Parade.	Menden.
"	0900-1100	Company in Attack	"
D.	0630-0730	Adjutant's Parade.	"
"	0900-1100	P.T., L.G., Grenades, &c.	"
		THURSDAY. *B Coy Route march* *D Coy Inoculation* *C : / 6 Cy C* *A*	
Battalion.		Route March.	
		FRIDAY.	
A.	0630-0730	Under O.C. Company.	Meindorf.
"	0900-1100	Outpost Duties.	Mendouf.
B.	0630-0730	R.S.Ms.Parade.	Menden
"	0900-1100	Coy in Defence.	do
C	1300-1800	Musketry	Range.
D	0600-1300	Musketry.	do
		SATURDAY.	
A	0630-0730	Saluting under O.C. Coy.	Meindorf.
B) C) D)	0630-0730	Saluting under R.S.M.	Bn Parade Ground
Battalion.	0915-1100	C.Os. Parade.	Bn Parade Ground.

26-7-19

Lieut Col Comdg.
51st Bn Manchester Regiment.

Army Form C. 2118.

51st March

WAR DIARY
or
INTELLIGENCE SUMMARY.
(Erase heading not required.)

Instructions regarding War Diaries and Intelligence Summaries are contained in F.S. Regs., Part II. and the Staff Manual respectively. Title pages will be prepared in manuscript.

AUGUST.

Place	Date	Hour	Summary of Events and Information	Remarks and references to Appendices
MENDEN	1/8/19		Training, Sports & Education programmes for week ending 9-8-19. App. HQrs A.T.C. taking disinfection of billets and clothing — changing blankets. D Coy on G.M.C. Great Irovation race to BIRLIN GHOVEN and back. "D"Coy Whey Drive Horses received 2323 lbs preparing dirts for move into new area at short notice. "C" Coy on G.M.C. "B" D'Lothing, disinfection of billets, clothing — changing blankets, also remainder of HQrs. A & C Coys.	A B + C
	2/8/19			A B + C
	3/8/19		Church Parade. Inf of an advanced party at GEISTINGEN. Orders received for Battalion to move to GEISTINGEN on 5th inst.	
	4/8/19		Bank Holiday — Training in Progress — Advanced parties read to take over New area at Geistingen. Billeting party from 10th Rifl Kents arrived to take over billets in Menden from us.	
	5/8/19		Battalion parade 0930 trs. & move to GEISTINGEN. Loading parties left behind for remains of stores and baggage, also for Brigade School Stores. Battalion under Canvas. Canvas and Brigade School Personnel attached for rations and accommodation.	
GEISTINGEN	6/8/19		Training under O.C. Companies. M.O's Inspection.	
	7/8/19		"A" Coy on Range for G.M.C. Battalion represented in Army Sports (3 miles) Relt 3rd & 4th. — Party of 1 Officer + 20 O.R. sent to BONRATH to relieve Platoon of 2nd BDE. dismantling tented camp.	
	8/8/19		"A" Coy G.M.C. — Supplied NIEDER PLEIS Guard. Battalion N.C.O's house commenced (ace C(w))	
	9/8/19		"A" Coy G.M.C. — Guard mounted at BDE. HDQRS. — Training. Sports and Education programme for week ending 16.8.19. (W) Visited left half Battn. + Rifle Ref.	
	10/8/19		Church Parade — "A" Coy on Range G.M.C.	

D. D. & L., London, E.C. Wt. W1771/M2031 750,000 5/17 Sch. 52 Forms/C2.16/14
(A8021) Forms/C2.16/14

WAR DIARY or INTELLIGENCE SUMMARY.

Army Form C. 2118.

AUGUST.

Place	Date	Hour	Summary of Events and Information	Remarks and references to Appendices
GEISINGEN	11/8/19		"A" Coy. G.M.C. (concluded) Platoon Cross Country Championships – No 13 plu. v 53rd Batt (best platoon) Result 51st won.	
	12/8/19		"B" Hd.Qrs & "C" Coys bathing – Afternoon "B" Coy on Range G.M.C. Examination on professional subjects for 2/Sgts & Cpls wishing to qualify for rank of Sergeant.	
	13/8/19		"B" Coy on Range G.M.C. Bathing D "A" & transport – Cricket Match at HENNEF v 53 Battalion. Result 53rd won. – Examinations on professional subjects for junior N.C.Os for promotion – Lt. Keen to Armee (strew) Corps Hqrs at NOYELLES.	
	14/8/19		"C" Coy continue G.M.C. Medical Inspection – Concert party of 15th–16th Lancashire Fusiliers performed 14th & 15th. Court of Inquiry at B.H.Q. reference loss of stores at NIEDER PLEIS dump. "B" Coy completed Part III G.M.C. Sent guards to NIEDER PLEIS and MENDEN to relieve those of "C" Coy. Inspection of listening here. Inspection of all Rewing Lorries.	
	15/8/19		"C" Coy on Range G.M.C. Training, Sports & Education programme for week ending 23/8/19 Brigade Platoon Cross Country Championship – Result 13 Platoon v best Platoon 63rd battalion. Result 51st won.	
	16/8/19		French Guards. "C" Coy on Range G.M.C. Officers Lecture v Officers of 53rd Battalion Result 53rd won.	
	17/8/19		"C" Coy. on Range – Part III G.M.C (concluded) "A" Coy struck off duties for Company training Sent 5 O.R. on visit to Ypres battlefields.	
	18/8/19		"A" Coy continued Company Training – Remainders under Company Commanders. Remainders returned to men & remainders sent to Chief Paymaster.	
	19/8/19 20/8/19		Pay Books of Battalion done during week. Will Platoons returned to men & remainders sent to Chief Paymaster.	

Army Form C. 2118.

WAR DIARY
or
INTELLIGENCE SUMMARY.
(Erase heading not required.)

AUGUST

Place	Date	Hour	Summary of Events and Information	Remarks and references to Appendices
GEISTINGEN	21/8/19		Paymaster, General Headquarters, Cologne, British Army of the Rhine. "A" Company continues training - Remainder under Company Commanders seeing to having men away on Guards, staying camps - guarding Ranges & Sports fields.	
	22/8/19		"A" Company continues training - Station of "D" Company returns from mending over "Borrath" family. Working party of 40 N.C.O.s & men under off. (Letherington) sent to Sports field & signing for work. Getting ready for Lancashire Division Horse Show. One man transferred to No. 8 Aux Ambulance Coy. 7 men to 93rd field training as usual. Ambulance also.	
	23/8/19		Orders received to move battalion out on Guards as follows - Lt. Galloway & 36 other ranks to Wahn - Lt. Mulholland & 46 other ranks to Dynamite factory Dues - 10 other ranks to Dye works. Walm - Lieutenant Walker one other officer and 49 other ranks to N.A.C.B. Sighing - Lt. Bergins & 14 other ranks to Borden factory Swisdorf - 15 other ranks to forest camp, Germers- Lt. Jamison 18 other ranks to R.T.O., Cologne - 3 other ranks to lectures Gloteau, Cologne. Lt. Renwick, Keaton & Taylor to Henry Central Bank, & 36 other ranks - Bn. Headquarters only remaining on Guestungon & commander of transport, Pioneers, Sanitary - Guards only.	
	24/8/19		Distribution as above carried out.	
	25/8/19		continued	
	26/8/19		do	
	27/8/19		do	
	28/8/19		Bn. still doing Guard duties	

Army Form C. 2118.

WAR DIARY
or
INTELLIGENCE SUMMARY.
(Erase heading not required.)

AUGUST

Place	Date	Hour	Summary of Events and Information	Remarks and references to Appendices
	29/8/19		53 men awarded 3rd Class Certificates of Education & second class. — Lt Col. H. S. Watson (M.S., A.S.O.) returned from leave to U.K.	
	30/8/19		Guard duties continued	
	31/8/19		do	

A. S. Watson
Lieut. Colonel.
Commanding 51st Bn. Manchester Regt

51st BN. THE MANCHESTER REGIMENT.

PROGRAMME OF TRAINING FOR WEEK ENDING AUGUST 9th, 1919.

A

Coy.	Time.	Nature of Training.	Place.

MONDAY.

Cancelled. Holiday. Preparations for Battalion move into Turstungen

Coy.	Time.	Nature of Training.	Place.
A.	0630-1300.	Musketry.	Range.
B.	1300-1800.	Musketry.	Range.
C.	0630-0730.	Adjutant's Parade.	Battalion Parade Ground
	0900-1100.	Flank Guard.	Menden.
D.	0630-0730.	Adjutant's Parade.	Battn. Parade Ground.
	0900-1100	Advanced Guard (Meeting Opposition)	" " "
Bn.	0800-1100.	N.C.O's Class.	

TUESDAY.

Battalion moved into Turstungen 0930hrs

A.	0630-0730.	R.S.M's Parade.	Battn. Parade Ground.
	0900-1100.	Reinforcing an A.G. which is held up.	Vicinity of Range.
B.	0630-0730.	R.S.M's Parade.	Battn. Parade Ground.
	0900-1100.	Moving through an A.G. and taking up Outpost position.	Vicinity of Range.
C.	0630-1300.	Musketry.	Range.
D.	1300-1800.	Musketry.	Range.
Bn.	0800-1100.	N.C.O's Class.	

WEDNESDAY.

0900-1100 Under OC Companies
1130-1230 Education
1400 - Kit Inspection

A.	1300-1800.	Musketry.	Range.
B.	0630-1300.	Musketry.	Range.
C.	0630-0730.	Adjutant's Parade.	Battn. Parade Ground.
	0900-1100.	Reinforcing an A.G. (held up)	Vicinity of Range.
D.	0630-0730.	Adjutant's Parade.	Battn. Parade Ground.
	0900-1100.	Moving through an A.G. and taking up Outpost position.	Vicinity of Range.
Bn.	0800-1100.	N.C.O's Class.	

THURSDAY.

A Coy - GMC
Remainder - Under OC's Coy

Bn.	0700-1230.	Route March.	

FRIDAY.

A Coy - GMC

A.	0630-0730.	R.S.M's Parade.	Battn. Parade Ground.
	0900-1100.	Moving through an A.G. and taking up Outpost position.	Vicinity of Range.
B.	0630-0730.	R.S.M's Parade.	Battn. Parade Ground.
	0900-1100.	Reinforcing an A.G. (held up)	Vicinity of Range.
C.	1300-1800.	Musketry.	Range.
D.	0630-1300.	Musketry.	Range.
Bn.	0800-1100.	N.C.O's Class.	

SATURDAY.

Bn.	0630-0730.	Saluting.	Battn. Parade Ground.
	0900-1100.	C.O's Parade.	" " "

1/8/19.

Major, Commdg.,
51st Bn. The Manchester Regiment.

51st Bn Manchester Regiment.

SPORTS PROGRAMME FOR WEEK ENDING 10th August.1919

DATE.	COY.	TIME.	PLACE.	NATURE OF SPORT.
3-8-19	51st Mancs. V 52nd Mancs	1500	Menden	Tug of war Div Compt 1st round.
4-8-19	Winners of No.4 Pltn & No.9 Pltn. V.Best Pltn.53rd Mancs.Regt.	1500	Menden	Soccer Final Bde. Pltn sports cup.
5-8-19	"C" Coy V "D" Coy	1430	do	Cricket.
6-8-19	No.13 Pltn V Best Pltn 53rd Mancs Regt.	1500	Geistingen	Semi-Final Cross Running in Bde Pltn Sports cup.
7-8-19	"C" Coy V Best Coy 52nd Mancs	1500	Menden	Soccer-Div. Compt. 1st round
8-8-19	51st MancsV 52nd & 53rd Mancs.	1500	Geistingen.	Cross-Country running Div Compt. about 5miles;Teams of 20.
9-8-19	Winner of Semi-Final on 6-8-19 V.52nd Mancs Regt.	1500	Rott & Freckwinkle Area.	Final Cross country Bde Pltn sports cup Compt.

1-8-19
(Sgnd.) G.S.Thwaits. Lieut,
Battalion Sports Officer.

1st Bn Manchester Regiment.

PROGRAMME OF EDUCATION TRAINING FOR WEEK ENDING AUGUST 9th 1919

DAY.	TIME.	COY.	SUBJECT.	INSTRUCTOR.
Mon.	1130-1230	A	Citizenship.	Lt Fryer.
"	" "	"	"C" Group Arithmetic.	Lt Murray.
"	" "	B	Arithmetic	Sgt Holden.
"	" "	"	"C" Group Arithmetic.	Sgt Wainwright.
"	" "	C	Geography	Sgt Taylor
"	" "	"	"C" Group Arithmetic	Pte Patterson.
"	" "	D	English	Lt Whiteside
"	" "	"	"C" Group Arithmetic	Sgt Steele
Tue.	1130-1230	A	Geography	Sgt Thornton.
"	" "	"	"C" Group English.	Lt Murray.
"	" "	B	Citizenship	Lt Fryer.
"	" "	"	"C" Group English	Sgt Wainwright.
"	" "	C	Citizenship	Lt Fryer
"	" "	"	"C" Group English	Pte Patterson.
"	" "	D	Citizenship	Lt Fryer
"	" "	"	"C" Group English	Sgt Steele
Wed	1130-1230	A	Gen Knowledge	Sgt Firth
"	" "	"	"C" Group Gen Knowledge	Sgt Thornton
"	" "	"	Geography	Sgt Smith
"	" "	"	"C" Group Gen Know.	" Wainwright
"	" "	C	English	Lt Whiteside
"	" "	"	C Group Eng Know.	Pte Paterson
"	" "	D	Arithmetic	Sgt Holden
"	" "	"	C" Group Gen. Know.	Sgt Steele.
Thurs.	" "	A	Arithmetic	Sgt Firth.
"	" "	"	C Group English.	Lieut. Murray.
"	" "	B	Debates.	Sgt Smith.
"	" "	"	C. Group English	Sgt Wainwright.
"	" "	C	Debate.	Lt Fryer.
"	" "	"	C Group English.	Pte Paterson.
"	" "	D	Debate.	Sgt Steele.
"	" "	"	D Group.	" "
Fri.	11-30-1230	A	Debate	Sgt Thornton.
"	" "	"	C Group Arithmetic.	Lt. Murray.
"	" "	B	English.	Sgt Smith.
"	" "	"	C Group Arithmetic.	" Wainwright.
"	" "	C	Arithmetic	" Holden
"	" "	"	C Group Arithmetic	Pte Paterson.
"	" "	D	Geography	Sgt Taylor.
"	" "	"	C Group Arithmetic.	" Steele.
Sat.	11-30-1230	A	English	Sgt Firth.
"	" "	"	" Group Gen Know.	" Thornton.
"	" "	B	Gen. Knowledge	" Smith
"	" "	"	" C Group Gen. Know.	" Wainwright
"	" "	C	Gen Knowledge	" Taylor
"	" "	"	" C Group Gen Know.	Pte Paterson.
"	" "	D	Gen. Knowledge	Sgt Holden.
"	" "	"	" C Group Gen. Know.	" Steele.

NOTE.

Citizenship Lecture for "B" "C" & "D" Companies on Tuesdays will be held in "D" Coys Messing Centre.

(Sgd) W. Mulholland
Education Officer

C (a)

N. C. O's CLASS.

Programme for Week Ending 16th August, 1919.

MONDAY.   0900-1000 hrs.   Drill (Secs. 1 - 24).
           1000-1100 "   P.T.
           1100-1200 "   B.T.
           1200-1230 "   Lecture (Musketry - Care of
                                     Arms - Theory).

TUESDAY.   0900-1000 hrs.   Drill (Secs. 25 - 46) 10 min. C.D.
           1000-1100 "   B.T.
           1100-1200 "   Musketry (Standing & Prone)
           1200-1230 "   Lecture. A/Adjt "Aiming Instruction"

WEDNESDAY. 0900-1000 hrs.   Drill (Secs. 47 - 58) 10 min. C.D.
           1000-1100 "   Musketry (Kneeling position).
           1100-1200 "   B.T.
           1200-1230 "   Lecture. "Interior Economy & Coy duties" RSM

THURSDAY. 0900-1000 hrs.   Drill (class taking) 10 min. C.D.
           1000-1100 "   Musketry (class taking).
           1100-1200 "   B.T.
           1200-1230 "   Lecture. Commanding Officer

FRIDAY.   0900-1000 hrs.   Drill (Secs. 59 - 74). 10 min. C.D.
           1000-1100 "   P.T.
           1100-1200 "   Musketry (Indictn. & Recgtn).
           1200-1230 "   Lecture. Major Wood MC "NCOs and Military Law"

SATURDAY. 0900-1000 hrs.   Drill (revision). 10 min. C.D.
           1000-1100 "   P.T.
           1100-1200 "   B.T.
           1200-1230 "   Lecture.

51st BN. THE MANCHESTER REGIMENT.

PROPOSED PROGRAMME OF TRAINING FOR WEEK ENDING 16/8/19.

MONDAY 11th.

A Coy.	All day.	Musketry, Part 3. Range.
B "	0700 hrs.	Rouse Parade - 0845-1000 hrs. P.T. & B.F. - 1000-1100 hrs Platoon Drill.
C "	0700 "	Arms Drill, 0845-1000 hrs. Musketry, 1000-1100 hrs B. Training.
D. "	0700 "	Rouse parade, 0845-1000 hrs. Musketry, 1000-1100 hrs P.T. & B.F.

N.C.O's Class 0900-1200 hrs Class work; 1400-1500 hrs Lectures.

TUESDAY.

A "	All day	Musketry, Part 3. Range.
B "	0700 hrs.	Rouse Parade; 0845-1000 hrs. Elementary Musketry, 1000-1100 hrs. Guard Drill.
C. "	0700 "	Rouse Parade; 0845-onwards Outposts.
D. "	0700 "	Rouse Parade; 0845-1000 P.T. & B.F; 1000-1100 hrs. Visual Training, etc.

N.C.O's Class. 0900-1200 & 1400-1500 hours.

WEDNESDAY.

A "	0700 hrs.	Rouse Parade, 0845-1100 L.G. Training, P.T. & B.F.
B "	All day.	Musketry. Range.
C "	0700 hrs.	Rouse Parade. 0845-1000 hrs. Extended Order and Artillery formation. 1000-1100 hrs. Platoon Drill.
D. "	0700 "	Rouse Parade, 0845-1000 P.T. & B.F.; 1000-1100 hrs Visual Training, etc.

N.C.O's Class. 0900-1200 & 1400-1500 hours.

THURSDAY.

A "	0630-0730 "	Handling of Arms, Platoon Drill, Ceremonial. 0900-1100 hrs. at disposal of O.C. Coy.
B "	All day.	Musketry Range.
C. "		Route March.
D "	0630-0730 "	Platoon Drill; 0900-1100 Coy Route march and small scheme.

N.C.O's Class 0900-1200 & 1400-1500 hours.

FRIDAY.

A. "	0630-0730 Hrs.	Saluting Drill. - 0900-1100 Initial stages of Company in attack.
B. "	All day	Musketry. Range
C "	0630-0730	Rouse Parade - 0900-1100 Advance Guards.
D "	0630-0700	Saluting Drill with and without arms - 0900-1100 hrs Musketry, P.T. & B.F.

N.C.O's Class 0900-1200 & 1400-1500 hrs.
Classwork. Lecture.

SATURDAY.

A "	0630-0730 hrs.	Arms drill and ceremonial. - 0900-1100 L.G. Training, P.T. & B.F.
B "	All day.	Musketry. Range.
C "	0630-0730 "	Rouse Parade. - 0900-1100 Company Drill.
D "	0630-0730 "	Arms Drill. - 0900-1100 Specialist training 2-1/2 hrs P.T.

N.C.O's Class 0900-1200 hrs Class work.
1400-1500 " Lecture.

(Sgd) G.W.Devlin, Major,
Commdg. 51st Bn. The Manchester Regiment.

9/8/19.

51st. BN. MANCHESTER REGIMENT.

SPORTS PROGAMME FOR WEEK ENDING 16th. AUGUST 1919.

Date.	Teams.	Time.	Place.	Nature of sport.
10-8-19.	N.C.O's v O.R's.	1430 hrs.	Geistingen.	Cricket.
11-8-19.	13 Ptn. v Best Ptn in 53rd. Bn. Manchester Rgt	1500 "	"	Semi-Final Cross Country Run. Bde Spor
12-8-19	"A"Coy. v "B"Coy.	1415 "	"	Cricket.
13-8-19	51st. Mans. v 53rd.	1430 "	Hennef.	"
14-8-19	"C"Coy. v "D"Coy.	1415 "	Geistingen	"
15-8-19	"A" & "B" Coys v. "C" & "D" Coys.	1430 "	"	"
16-8-19	Battalion.	1430 "	"	Paper Chase.

9-8-1919.

(Sgd) J.R. Penswick, Lieut.
Sports Officer,
51st. Bn. The Manchester Regiment.

51st BN. THE MANCHESTER REGT.

Programme of Education Training for Week Ending August 16th 1919.

Day.	Time.	Coy.	Subject.	Instructor.
Mon.	1130-1230	A.	Citizenship.	Lieut. Fryer.
"	"	"	"C" Group Arithmetic.	" Murray,
"	"	"	B. Arithmetic.	Sgt. Holden,
"	"	"	" "C" Group Arithmetic.	" Wainwright.
"	"	"	" "C" Group Arithmetic.	" Taylor,
"	"	"	C. Geography,	Pte. Paterson,
"	"	"	" "C" Group Arithmetic.	Lieut. Whiteside.
"	"	"	D. English,	Sgt. Steele.
"	"	"	" "C" Group Arithmetic.	
Tue.	1130-1230	A.	Geography,	Sgt. Thornton.
"	"	"	" "C" Group English,	Lt. Murray.
"	"	"	B Citizenship,	Lt. Fryer,
"	"	"	" "C" Group English	Sgt. Wainwright.
"	"	"	C Citizenship	Lt. Fryer.
"	"	"	" "C" Group English,	Pte. Paterson,
"	"	"	D Citizenship,	Lt. Fryer,
"	"	"	" "C" Group English.	Sgt. Steele.
Wed.	1130-1230	A.	Gen. Knowledge.	Sgt. Firth.
"	"	"	" "C" Group Gen. Knowledge	Sgt. Thornton.
"	"	"	B Geography,	" Smith.
"	"	"	" "C" Group Gen.Knowledge.	" Wainwright.
"	"	"	C English,	Lt. Whiteside.
"	"	"	" "C" Group EnglishGen.Kno.	Pte. Paterson.
"	"	"	D Arithmetic.	Sgt. Holden.
"	"	"	" "C" Group Gen. Know.	" Steele.
Thu.	1130-1230	A.	Arithmetic.	Sgt. Firth.
"	"	"	" "C" Group English	Lt. Murray,
"	"	"	B. Debates,	Sgt. Smith.
"	"	"	" "C" Group English,	" Wainwright.
"	"	"	C Debate.	Lt. Fryer.
"	"	"	" "C" Group English.	Pte. Paterson.
"	"	"	D Debate.	Sgt. Steele.
"	"	"	" "C" Group English.	" "
Fri.	1130-1230	A.	Debate.	Sgt. Thornton,
"	"	"	" "C" Group Arithmetic.	Lt. Murray,
"	"	"	B English	Sgt. Smith.
"	"	"	" "C" Group Arithmetic.	" Wainwright.
"	"	"	C Arithmetic.	" Holden.
"	"	"	" "C" Group Arithmetic	Pte. Paterson.
"	"	"	D. Geography,	Sgt. Taylor.
"	"	"	" "C" Group Arithmetic.	" Steele.
Sat.	1130-1230	A.	English.	Sgt. Firth.
"	"	"	" "C" Group Gen.Knowledge.	" Thornton.
"	"	"	B. General Knowledge.	" Smith.
"	"	"	" "C" Group Gen. Knowledge.	" Wainwright.
"	"	"	C. General Knowledge,	" Taylor.
"	"	"	" "C" Group Gen.Knowledge.	Pte. Paterson.
"	"	"	D. General Knowledge.	Sgt. Holden.
"	"	"	" "C" Group Gen. Knowledge.	" Steele.

NOTE.

Citizenship Lecture for "B", "C" and "D" Companies on Tuesday will be held in "D" Coy's Messing Centre.

(Sgd) W. Mullholland,
Education Officer.

51st BN. THE MANCHESTER REGIMENT.

Programme of Training for Week ending August 23rd 1919.

Coy.	Time.	Nature of Training.	Location.
MONDAY			
A.	0630-0730 hrs.	Organization of Coy.	Camp.
	0900-1100 "	(Demonstration & Practice of Battle) Order and Full Marching Order.	"C" Coy on Range GMC
B.	0630-0730 "	Platoon Drill.	Camp.
	0900-1100 "	(0900-1000) hrs. P.T. & B.F.) (1000-1100 " Musketry & L.G.)	"
C.	0630-0730 "	Arms Drill.	"
	0900-1100 "	Musketry & B.F.	"
D.	0630-0730 "	Platoon Drill.	"
	0900-1100 "	Musketry & B.F.	"
TUESDAY			
A.	0630-0730 hrs.	Company Drill.	Camp.
	0900-1100 "	(Advance Guard, Company Artillery) (Formation.	Geistingen.
B.	0630-0730 "	Saluting Drill.	Camp.
	0900-1100 "	Advance Guards	Geistingen.
C.	0630-0730 "	Saluting Drill.	Camp.
	0900-1100 "	Outposts.	Geistingen.
D.	0630-0730 "	Arms Drill.	Camp.
	0900-1100 "	P.T. & B.F., Visual Training.	"
WEDNESDAY			
A.	0630-0730 hrs.	Company Ceremonial.	Camp.
	0900-1100 "	Initial Stages of Attack.	Geistingen.
B.	0630-0730 "	Arms Drill.	Camp.
	0900-1100 "	Extended Order Drill.	Geistingen.
C.	0630-0730 "	Company Drill.	Camp.
	0900-1100 "	Extended Order & Platoon Drill.	Geistingen.
D.	0630-0730 "	Musketry.	Camp.
	0900-1100 "	Guard Drill & Musketry.	"
THURSDAY			
A.	0630-0730 hrs.	Company Drill.	Camp.
	0900-1100 "	Later Stages of Attack.	Geistingen.
B.	0630-0730 ")	Route March.	
	0900-1100 ")		
C.	0630-0730 ")	Route March.	
	0900-1100 ")		
D.	0630-0730 "	Platoon Drill.	Camp.
	0900-1100 "	Route March & Small Scheme.	
FRIDAY			
A.	0630-0730 hrs.	Company Drill.	Camp.
	0900-1100 "	Consolidation of Position & Defence.	Place to be reconnoitred.
B.	0630-0730 "	Company Drill.	Camp.
	0900-1000 "	Gas Drill.	"
	1000-1100 "	Guard Drill.	"
C.	0630-0730 "	Arms Drill.	"
	0900-1100 "	Advance Guards.	Geistingen.
D.	0630-0730 "	Saluting Drill (with & without arms)	Camp.
	0900-1100 "	Musketry, P.T. & B.F.	"
SATURDAY			
A.	0630-0730 hrs.	Company Drill.	Camp.
	0900-1100 "	Company in complete Attack. Place to be reconnoitred.	
B.	0630-0730 "	Company Drill.	Camp.
	0900-1100 "	Specialist Training	"
C.	0630-0730 "	Platoon Drill.	"
	0900-1100 "	Company Drill.	"
D.	0630-0730 "	Arms Drill.	"
	0900-1100 "	Specialist Training with ½ hr's P.T.	"

N.C.O's Class daily 0900-1200 hrs. Lecture 1200-1230 hrs. Medical Inspection Thursday 1430 hours. Kit Inspection and changing clothing. Friday 1430 hrs.

(Sgd) G.TWIGG, Capt.& Adj

15/8/19.

51st Bn. The Manchester Regiment.

J.

N. C. O's CLASS.

Programme for Week Ending 23rd August, 1919.

MONDAY.   0900-1000 hrs. Drill (Secs. 75 - 80 platoon drill)
                            10 min. C.D.
             1000-1100 "   P.T.)
             1100-1200 "   B.T.) class taking (half classes).
             1200-1230 "   Lecture - Drill. *Adjutant*

TUESDAY.   0900-1000 hrs. Drill (revision & questions). 10 min. C.D.
             1000-1100 "   Musketry (rapid aim and load).
             1100-1200 "   B.T.
             1200-1230 "   Lecture. *a/adj' "Use & mis-use of cover"*

WEDNESDAY.   0900-1000 hrs. Drill (Guard duties)   C.D.
             1000-1100 "   P.T.
             1100-1200 "   Musketry, F.D. (1 & 2).
             1200-1230 "   Lecture. *Commanding Officer*

THURSDAY.   0900-1000 hrs. Drill (platoon drill & class taking).
             1000-1100 "   B.T.
             1100-1200 "   Musketry (F.D. (3).).
             1200-1230 "   Lecture. *Major Wood MC "The NCO in the field and in action"*

FRIDAY.   0900-1000 hrs. Drill (class taking) C.D.
             1000-1100 "   P.T.
             1100-1200 "   Musketry (class taking).
             1200-1230 "   Lecture. *Commanding Officer*

SATURDAY.   0900-1000 hrs. Drill (class taking) C.D.
             1000-1100 "   B.T.
             1100-1200 "   Musketry (class taking).
             1200-1230 "   Lecture. *a/adj' "Range discipline"*

51st. BN. MANCHESTER REGIMENT.

SPORTS PROGRAMME FOR WEEK ENDING 23rd. AUGUST 1919.

Date.	Teams.	Time.	Place.	Nature of Sport.
17-8-19	51st Mans. V	1415 hrs.	Nennef	Cricket.
18-	53rd, Mancs.			
18-8-19.	Officers V O.R.	1430 "	Geistingen.	Tug of War.
19-8-19.	"C " Coy V "A" Coy.	1715 "	"	Football.
20-8-19.	B " D "	1430 "	"	Cricket.
21-8-19.	"C" Coy V "A" Coy	1430 "	"	"
22-8-19.	"A" & "B" V "C" & "D"	1430 hrs.	"	"
23-8-19.	Officers V. Other Ranks	1430 hrs.	Geistingen	"

(Sgd) J. R. Penswick Lieut
Sports Officer.
51st, Bn, The Manchester
Regiment.

51st BN. MANCHESTER REGIMENT.

PROGAMME OF EDUCATIONAL TRAINING FOR WEEK ENDING 23rd AUGUST 1919

Day	Time	Coy.	Subject	Instructor
Monday	11:30-12:30	"A & B"	Citizenship.	Lieut. Fryer.
"	"	" "	"C" Group Arithmetic.	" Murray.
"	"	"C & D"	English.	" Whiteside.
"	"	" "	"C" Group Arithmetic.	Sgt. Steele.
Tuesday	"	" "A & B"	Geography.	" Thornton.
"	"	" "	"C" Group English.	Lieut. Murray.
"	"	" "C & D"	Geography.	Sgt. Smith.
"	"	" "	"C" Group English.	" Steele.
Wednesday.	"	" "A & B"	English.	Lieut. Whiteside.
"	"	" "	"C" Group Gen. Knowledge	" Murray.
"	"	" "C & D"	Citizenship.	" Fryer.
"	"	" "	"C" Group. Gen. Knowledge.	Sgt. Steele.
Thursday.	"	" "A & B"	Arithmetic.	" Firth.
"	"	" "	"C" Group.	Lieut. Murray.
"	"	" "C & D"	Aritjmetic.	Sgt. Thornton.
"	"	" "	"C" Group English.	" Steele.
Friday.	"	" "A & B"	Debate. /Debate./	Sgt. Smith.
"	"	" "	"C" Group.	Sgt. Smith.
"	"	" "C & D"	Debate.	Sgt. Steele.
"	"	" "	"C" Group Debate.	" "
Saturday.	"	" "A & B"	Gen. Knowledge.	" Firth.
"	"	" "	"C" Group Arithmetic.	Lieut. Whiteside.
"	"	" "C & D"	Gen.Knowledge.	Sgt. Smith.
"	"	" "	"C" Group.Arithmetic.	" Thornton.

GEISTINGTON.
15-8-19.

(Sgd.) D. Whiteside.
For Education Officer,
51st Bn. Manchester Regt.

51st Bn. The Lanchester Regiment.

PROGRAMME OF EDUCATIONAL TRAINING. FOR WEEK ENDING 30-8-1919.

Day.	Time.	Coy.	Subject.	Instructor.
Monday.	1130-1230	"A"	Arithmetic.	Sergt. Thornton.
"	"	"B"	English.	Lieut. Whiteside.
"	"	"A & B"	C Group - Arithmetic	Sergt. Firth.
"	"	"C & D"	" English History.	Sgt. Smith.
"	"	"C"	C Group - Arithmetic	Sergt. Paterson.
"	"	"D"	" "	" Steele.
Tuesday.	1130-1230	A & B	Citizenship.	Lieut. Mulholland.
"	"	A & B	C Group. - English.	Sergt. Firth.
"	"	C	Arithmetic.	Sergt. Thornton.
"	"	C	C Group. - English.	Sergt. Paterson.
"	"	D	English.	Lieut. Whiteside.
"	"	D	C Group. - English.	Sergt. Steele.
Wednesday.	"	A & B	Geography.	Sergt. Smith.
"	"	do.	C Group. - General Knowledge.	" Firth.
"	"	C	English.	Lieut. Whiteside.
"	"	C	C Group. - General Knowledge	Sgt. Paterson.
"	"	D	Arithmetic.	Sergt Thornton.
"	"	D	C Group. - General Knowledge	" Steele.
Thursday.	"	A & B	English History.	Sergt. Smith.
"	"	"	C Group. - Arithmetic.	Sergt. Firth.
"	"	C & D	Citizenship.	Lieut. Mulholland.
"	"	C	C Group. - Arithmetic.	Sergt. Steele.
"	"	D	" do.	Sergt. Paterson.
Friday.	"	A & B	Debate.) includes C	Sergt. Smith.
"	"	C & D	Debate.) Group.	Lieut. Fryer.
Saturday.	"	A	English.	Lieut. Whiteside.
"	"	B	Arithmetic.	Sergt. Thornton.
"	"	A & B	C Group. - English.	Sergt. Firth.
"	"	C & D	Geography.	Sergt. Smith.
"	"	C	C Group. - English.	Sergt. Paterson.
"	"	D	C Group. - English.	Sergt. Steele.

Geistingen,
21st August 1919.

(signed) W. MULHOLLAND, Lieut.
Education Officer,
51st Bn. The Lanchester Regiment.

Army Form C. 2118.

WAR DIARY
or
INTELLIGENCE SUMMARY.
(Erase heading not required.)

51st Tyneside Regt

Place	Date	Hour	Summary of Events and Information	Remarks and references to Appendices
	1/9/19		Bn Assembled at Monday, Guards at hrs. When leaving relieved by 10th Bn the Queens Regiment. Tyneside regiment from us by the 52nd Bn. the demobilisation beginning.	
	2/9/19		Bn settled down Billets	
	3/9/19			
	4/9/19 5/9/19 6/9/19		Training continued HQs & Co.'s parades	
	7/9/19		Bn Whist Drive held at 1830 hours —	
	8/9/19		Sunday. Divine Service. Stop meeting held. Lieut Mulholland M.C. & 13 ORs proceeded to demobilisation. B Company struck off duty & Training Part III of the S.M.E. remainder training as usual.	
	9/9/19		Capts Hunter & Davis & 15 ORanks proceed to Demobilisation. B Coy. musketry part III. June Training as usual. Conf. Officer presides at Summary Court for trial of German civilian accused — Training programme for week attached —	7 A.B.C.

WAR DIARY or INTELLIGENCE SUMMARY

Army Form C. 2118.

(Erase heading not required.)

Instructions regarding War Diaries and Intelligence Summaries are contained in F. S. Regs., Part II. and the Staff Manual respectively. Title pages will be prepared in manuscript.

Place	Date	Hour	Summary of Events and Information	Remarks and references to Appendices
MENDEN	10/9/19		D Coy on Range (Part III G.M.C.) Commanding Officer on Court Martial in Bonn. Personal General visited area, inspected Stores, Reception Room & Headquarters Coy Messing Hall. H.Q. Personnel with segregated returns to Battalion for duty. Sports & Education Programme for week-ending 13.9.19 issuing.	D E F
	11/9/19		A & G Coy on Range for Practice Shot prior to commencement of G.M.C. Battalion Route March and Advanced Guard scheme – 6 p.m. Divisional Coy Football Comptn "C" Coy v M.G.C. Medical Inspection –	
	12/9/19		H.Q. Coy commence G.M.C., remainder Coy's parade scheme – Inauguration of Flemish A & B Coys practice A & B Coys practice today – Events – Evening Girls Schs Pk Programme W.F. 209/19 MENDEN Leaving Inspection – for Medical Inspection from Burgomaster, MENDEN Jr. Received letter of thanks from Burgomaster at the new Town Appt assistance rendered by the Regiment at the Parade – Blankets	G H I J J(a)
	13/9/19		H.Q. Coy on Range (G.M.C.) – Commanding Officers Parade – Blankets of C, D & H.Q. Coy Fumigated. Brigade Orders in "D" Coy Evening Cinema – 2/Lt J Musgrove admitted to Hospital	

Army Form C. 2118.

WAR DIARY
or
INTELLIGENCE SUMMARY.
(Erase heading not required.)

Place	Date	Hour	Summary of Events and Information	Remarks and references to Appendices
MENDEN	14/9/19		Church Parade - 2nd O.C. on Range (S.M.C.) Bearers of Transport Inspected - Commanding Officer at Brigade Commander's Conference at GEISTINGEN re reorganisation of Battalion - Cricket match vs HENNEF v 53rd Battalion	
	15/9/19		HQ Coy on Range for entrainment of O.M.C. - Company training - Bathing. HQ Coy & A Coy & Transport - Authority received to send 34 O.R. to CONCENT (Concern) under G.R.O. 321 - Details Despatch Knock-out competition. 52nd - 51st in won -	
	16/9/19		HQ Coy on Range (S.M.C.) Bathing for remainder of Battn. Annual Cross Country Team Championship Competition. - 34 O.R. to RIEHL for Army Championship to CONCENT today.	
	17/9/19		HQ Coy complete S.M.C. - Disinfector Holden A B C & D Coys by Personnel Sunday Section - Medical Inspector - 2/Lt T.H. TRANNER to CONCENT today	
	18/9/19		Brigade Reorganisation - Army Game as RIEHL Cross country team (representing X Corps) competing	

Army Form C. 2118.

WAR DIARY
or
INTELLIGENCE SUMMARY.
(Erase heading not required.)

Place	Date	Hour	Summary of Events and Information	Remarks and references to Appendices
MENDEN	18/9/19		Disinfection of HQ Coy & Transport Lines – 30 O.R's to CORCENT today under GRO 321.	
	19/9/19		Coys on Interior Economy – First inspection re: new new amalgamation & reorganisation of Battalion – Battalion to be reduced by 2 Companies "D" is to be amalgamated with "A" and "C" with "B" – Coys marked for M.C. in command of Coys app 3 – To take effect on Sunday 21st inst. Leaving Coys in Educational Programme for week ending 27.9.19 app 3 {K/L {M	N
			20 O.R's proceeded to CORCENT today	
	20/9/19		Commanding Officers Parade & Games Instruction – Brigade Games mounted at Bdr. HQ – 2/Lt W.J. LECH 15th proceeded to CORCENT today – Orders formulated & issued reference parade civil disturbance and action by military if required	O
	21/9/19		Church Parade – New Battalion organisation takes from today.	
	22/9/19		Educational examinations for 2nd and 3rd class subjects to Bathing – Transport – "HQ" & "A" Coys – Authority received for	

(Ag173) Wt W2358/P360 60,000 12/17 D. D. & L. Sch. Bn. Forms/C2118/15.

Army Form C. 2118.

WAR DIARY
or
INTELLIGENCE SUMMARY.
(Erase heading not required.)

Instructions regarding War Diaries and Intelligence Summaries are contained in F.S. Regs., Part II. and the Staff Manual respectively. Title pages will be prepared in manuscript.

Place	Date	Hour	Summary of Events and Information	Remarks and references to Appendices
MINDEN	22/9/19		Officers complete to establishment. Battalion competing in Aquatic Sports. Stadium Boxing Competition (Brigade) at HENNEF. 1/52nd Battalion led platoon. 51st bn platoon winners. Remainder Education programme for week ending 27-9-19 app.	P
	23/9/19		Cadres of HQ, A + two D Coys firing GMC. Archery B Coy and men not in this yesterday – Lewis Coy. Honoured proceeded to Concert as anyhow to establishment – Divisional Aquatic Sports finals – month of Battalion competition 2 firsts, 4 seconds, I think –	
	24/9/19		Training suspended – Brigade Sports – heaves 51st bn winners of Cup for highest number of points – Brigade platoon Sports Cup presented to No 13 platoon –	
	25/9/19		Battalion Rhine Cup – 2/Lt J.R. McBryde proceeds to CONCERT today, together with 10 oth.	QR
	26/9/19		5 O.R. proceeded to CONCERT – Cadres of HQ, A + D Coys GMC.– Training, Sports & Education Programme for week ending 4-10-19 Brigade lecture showing in Battalion area	R S

Army Form C. 2118.

WAR DIARY
or
INTELLIGENCE SUMMARY.
(Erase heading not required.)

Instructions regarding War Diaries and Intelligence Summaries are contained in F. S. Regs., Part II. and the Staff Manual respectively. Title pages will be prepared in manuscript.

Place	Date	Hour	Summary of Events and Information	Remarks and references to Appendices
MENDEN	27/9/19		Cmds of HQ, A & D Coys G.M.C. – Instructors & staff of Brigade School commenced duty with Battalion upon school impairing. 1 Sgt. Maj. Glover reported for duty with battalion for 2 weeks, training Junior Officers, Senior NCOs in PT & BT –	
	28/9/19		Church parade –	
	29/9/19		Cmds of HQ, A & D Coys on Part III G.M.C. – Remainder training as per programme – Officers beat Sergeants – Rugby trial football – Officers' concert party in for selection of battalion team. 1730 hrs – Officers' concert party in Recreation Room 2000 hrs – Bathing – Transport & T.M. Coy	
	30/9/19		Cmds of HQ, A & D Coys (Part III) Remainder as per programme – Organise Boxing competition (2 competitors each batt. at 6 weights) at GEISTINGEN. – Bathing HQ & B Coy by air crowds.	

A Whatton Lt Col.

21st Bn Manchester Regiment.

PROGRAMME OF TRAINING FOR WEEK ENDING SEPT.6th 1919

Coy.	Time.	Nature of Training.	Place.

MONDAY.

| Bn. | All day. | Move to Menden. | |

TUESDAY.

| Bn. | All day. | Getting Messing centres, Latrines, Cookhouses, Billets cleaned. | Menden |

WEDNESDAY.

B&C Coys	0630-0730	Under Coy Comdrs.	Menden.
do	0930-1130	do do do	do
A Coy	0630-0730	Field Training.	do
do	0930-1130	do do	do
D.Coy.	All day.	Musketry G.M.C.	Range.

THURSDAY.

A.Coy.	0630-0730	Field Training.	Menden.
do	0930-1130	do do	do
B&C Coys	0630-0730	Under Coy Comdrs.	do
do	0930-1130	do do do	do
D.Coy.	All day.	Musketry G.M.C.	Range.

FRIDAY.

A.Coy.	0630-0730	Field Training.	Menden
do	0930-1130	do do	do
B&C Coys	0630-0730	Under Coy Comdrs.	do
do	0930-1130	do do do	do
D.Coy.	0630-0730		
	3 onwards	Musketry G.M.C.	Range.

SATURDAY.

A.Coy	0630-0730	Field Training.	Menden.
do	0930-1130	do do	do
B&C Coys	0630-0730	Under Coy Comdrs.	do
do	0930-1130	do do do	do
D.Coy.	All day.	Musketry G.M.C.	Range.

(Sgnd.) H.E.Watson. Lieut Col.
Comdg. 21st Bn.Manchester Regiment.

Sports   B

1st. Bn. THE MANCHESTER REGIMENT.

Date.	Coy.	Time.	Place.	Nature of Sport
1-9-1919.	----	All Day.	Move to London.	
2-9-1919.	"C" V "A"	1430. Hrs.	London.	Soccer.
3-9-1919.	"D" V "B"	" " " "	"	Cricket.
4-9-1919.	Battalion.	" "	"	Hockey Prac.
5-9-1919.	Winner "D&B" V "A"	" "	"	Cricket.
6-9-1919.	Hqrs V "B" Ptn.	" "	"	Soccer.
7-9-1919.	(Officers V rest of (Battalion.	" "	"	Cricket.

30-8-1919.

(Sgd) G.S.THWAITE.
Sports Officer.
1st. Bn. The Manchester Regt.

> H.Q.,
> LANCASHIRE DIVISION
> "A."
> A109
> 10/9/19

Lancashire Division.

G.I. 144

        Reference your A. 109 dated 6th September 1919.

        Original copy herewith.

                Lieut Colonel,
Commanding 3rd Manchester Infantry Bde.

9/9/1919.

1st. Bn. THE MANCHESTER REGIMENT.

PROGRAMME OF EDUCATIONAL TRAINING FOR WEEK ENDING 6th. September 1919.

Day.	Time.	Coy.	Subject.	Instructor.
Monday.	1130-1230.	"A"	Arithmetic	Sgt Thornton.
"	"	"B"	English	Lieut Whiteside.
"	"	"A & B"	"C" Group Arithmetic	Sgt Firth.
"	"	"C & D"	"C" Group English History	" Smith.
"	"	"C"	"C" Group Arithmetic	" Paterson.
"	"	"D"	" " "	" Steele.
Tuesday.	"	"A & B"	Citizenship	Lieut Mullholland
"	"	"	"C" Group English.	Sgt Firth.
"	"	"C"	Arithmetic	" Thornton.
"	"	"	"C" Group English	" Paterson.
"	"	"D"	English	Lieut Whiteside.
"	"	"	"C" Group English	Sgt Steele.
Wednesday.	"	"A & B"	Geography.	Sgt Smith.
"	"	"	"C" Group Gen. Knowledge	" Firth.
"	"	"C"	English.	Lieut Whiteside.
"	"	"	"C" Group Gen. Knowledge.	Sgt Paterson.
"	"	"D"	Arithmetic	" Thornton.
"	"	"C"	General Knowledge	" Steele.
Thursday.	"	"A & B"	English History	Sgt Smith.
"	"	"	"C" Group Arithmetic	" Firth.
"	"	"C & D"	Citizenship	Lieut Mullholland
"	"	"C"	"C" Group Arithmetic	Sgt Steele.
"	"	"D"	" " "	" Paterson.
Friday.	"	"A & B"	Debate.) Includes (	Sgt Smith.
"	"	"C & D"	Debate.) "C" Group. (	Lieut Fryer.
Saturday.	"	"A"	English.	Lieut Whiteside
"	"	"B"	Arithmetic.	Sgt Thornton.
"	"	"A & B"	"C" Group English.	" Firth.
"	"	"C & D"	Geography.	" Smith.
"	"	"C"	"C" Group English	" Paterson.
"	"	"D"	" " "	" Steele.

GöTTINGEN.
27-8-1919.

(Sgd) P. Fryer, Lieut

For Education Officer,
1st. Bn. THE MANCHESTER REGT.

SPORTS PROGRAMME FOR WEEK ENDING 13TH SEPTEMBER.

DATE.	COY.	TIME.	PLACE.		NATURE OF SPORT.
7-9-19.	"C" Coy V Rest Of Battn.	1500hrs	Menden		Soccer.
8-9-19.	Battalion	1800hrs	"		X Country Run.
9-9-19.	"C" V "D"	1500hrs	"	B Ground.	Soccer.
	"A" V "B"	1500 hrs		A "	Soccer.
10-9-19.	51st V 51st Kings	1430 hrs		A "	"
11-9-19	Officers V Rest Battn.	1430 hrs		B "	Cricket.
12-9-19.	Battalion.	1900hrs	Menden.		Dance in "L" Coy Mess Room.
"		1430hrs.	"		Cricket Practice.
13-9-19.	Battalion.	1600 hrs.	"		Battalion Practice Match.

(Sgd) G. Thwaites,
Sports Officer
51st, Bn, The Manchester Regt.

TRAINING PROGRAMME FOR WEEK-ENDING SEPT. 13TH 1919.

MONDAY.

"D" Coy.	All-day.	G. M. C.	Range. Menden.
Remainder	0630-0730	Adjutant's Parade	Drill. "
"	0930-1130	C. O.'s Parade	Drill "

TUESDAY.

Battalion.	0630-0730	R. S. M.'s Parade.	Menden.
"	0930-1130	C. O.'s Parade. Drill.	Menden.

WEDNESDAY.

"D" Coy.	All-day.	G. M. C.	Range. Menden.
Remainder	0630-0730	Adjutant's Parade.	Arms Drill Menden.
"	0930-1130	C. O.'s Parade.	Drill "

THURSDAY.

Battalion.	0630-0730	R. S. M.'S Parade.	Menden.
"	0930-1130	C. O.'S Parade.	Drill. Menden.

FRIDAY.

"D" Coy.	All-day	G. M. C.	Range Menden.
Remainder	0630-0730	Adjutant's Parade.	Battn, Drill Menden.
"	0930-1130	C. O.'S Parade	Drill "

SATURDAY.

Battalion.	0630-0730	R. S. M.'S Parade.	Saluting. Menden.
"	0930-1130	C. O.'S Parade.	Drill. "

NOTE.

Owing to the large number of N.C.O.'s and men on leave Coys are too weak to carry out Coy Training –

Education. 1145-1245 daily. Baths Monday and Tuesday.

Medical Inspection Thursdays.

(Sgd) H.F.Watson
Lieut,-Colonel,
Commanding, 51st, Bn, The Manchester Regt.

51st, Bn. The Manchester Regiment.

PROGRAMME OF EDUCATIONAL TRAINING FOR WEEK ENDING 13th, SEPTEMBER 1919.

DAY.	TIME.	COY.	SUBJECT.	INSTRUCTOR.
Monday.	1130-1230	A and B	Citizenship	Lieut, Mullholland.
"	"	A.	C Group Arith.	Sgt Firth.
"	"	B.	C " "	Sgt Taylor.
"	"	C,	English.	Lieut, Whiteside.
"	"	C	C Group Arithmetic	Sgt Paterson.
"	"	D.	Arithmetic	Sgt Steele.
"	"	D	C Group Arithmetic	" Holden.
Tuesday.	1130-1230	"A"	English	Lieut, Murray.
"	"	A	C.Group English	Sgt Firth.
"	"	B	Arithmetic	" Smith.
"	"	B	C Group English	" Taylor.
"	"	C and D.	Citizenship.	Lieut Mullholland.
"	"	C.	C Group English	Sgt Paterson.
"	"	D.	C Group "	" Holden.
Wednesday	1130-1230	A.	Arithmetic	Lieut, Murray.
"	"	A	C Group Gen Know.	Sgt Firth.
"	"	B.	English	" Smith.
"	"	B	C Group Gen Know.	" Taylor.
"	"	C	Arithmetic	Lieut, Whiteside.
"	"	C	C Group Gen Know.	Sgt Paterson,
"	"	D.	English	" Steele.
"	"	D. C Group Gen Know.		" Holden.
Thursday.	1130-1230	A. English		Lieut, Murray.
"	"	A C Group Arithmetic		Sgt Firth.
"	"	B. Arithmetic		" Smith.
"	"	B.C Group Arithmetic		" Taylor.
"	"	C English		Lieut, Whitesidez
"	"	C. C Group Arithmetic		Sgt Paterson.
"	"	D. Arithmetic		" Steele.
"	"	D. C Group Arithmetic		" Holden.
Friday,	1130-1230	A Arithmetic		Lieut, Murray.
"	"	A. C. Group Arithmetic		Sgt Firth.
"	"	B. English		" Smith.
"	"	B. C. Group Gen, Know.		" Taylor.
"	"	C. Arithmetic,		Lieut, Whiteside.
"	"	C. C.Group Gen Know.		Sgt Paterson.
"	"	D. English		" Steele.
"	"	D. C.Group Gen Know.		" Holden.
Saturday.	1130-1230	A.) B.) C.) D.)	TEST EXAMINATION. ENGLISH.	ALL INSTRUCTORS.

(Sgd) W.Mullholland,
Education Officer.
51st, Bn, The Manchester Reg

51st Bn Manchester Regiment.

TRAINING PROGRAMME FOR WEEK ENDING SEPTEMBER 20th 1919

Day.	Time.	Nature of Training.	Place	Range.
15-9-19		H.Q.Coy G.M.C.		Range Mendon
"	0630-0730	Adjts Parade		Mendon
"	0930-1015	C.O. Parade. Bn Drill		"
"	10-15-1130	Coy Drill, Arms Drill		"
		HQ GMC.		
16-9-19	0630-0730	R.S.M.Parade.		Mendon
"	0930-1015	C.O. Parade.		"
"	1015-1130	Extended Order Artillery Formation		"
17-9-19		H.Q.Coy G.M.C.		Mendon
"	0630-0730	Adjts Parade		"
"	0930-1015	C.O.Parade		"
"	1015-1130	Pltn Drill & Guard Drill		"
18-9-19	0630-0730	R.S.M.Parade	Army Sports	Mendon
"	0930-1130	Bn Route March & Scheme		"
19-9-19		H.Q.Coy G.M.C.	Kit inspection &	Range Mendon
"	0630-0730	Adjts Parade	amalgamation of Coys.	Mendon
"	0930-1015	C.O.Parade		"
"	1015-1130	Coy in attack.		
20-9-19	0630-0730	R.S.M.Parade		Mendon
"	0930-1015	C.O.Parade		"
"	1015-1130	Outpost Scheme		"

NOTE.

Education 1145-1245 daily. Bathing Monday & Tuesday.
Medical Inspection Thursday.

11-9-19

(Sgnd.) H.F.Watson Lieut Col.
Condg. 51st Bn Manchester Regiment.

51st Bn Manchester Regiment.

SPORTS PROGRAMME FOR WEEK ENDING SEPTEMBER 20th 1919

DATE.	COY.	TIME.	PLACE	NATURE OF SPORT.
14-9-19	51st Manch Regt. V. 53rd Manch Regt.	1400	Hennef	Cricket.
15-9-19	"A" Coy V. "B" Coy.	1400hrs or 1800 hrs	Menden	Football
16-9-19	"C" Coy V. "D" Coy	do	do	do
17-9-19	Battalion	1400	P. & R.T.School	Cross Country (20 Runners)
18-9-19			Richl	Army Athletic Championships
19-9-19	H.Q.Coy V "B" Coy	1400	Menden	Cricket
20-9-19	No.4 Pltn V.No 5 Pltn	1600	Menden	Football

11-9-19

(Sgnd.) G.S.Thwaits. Lieut.
Battalion Sports Officer.

21st Bn Manchester Regiment.

PROGRAMME OF EDUCATIONAL TRAINING FOR WEEK ENDING 20th Sept. 1919

INSTRUCTORS.

Monday till Saturday. 1145-1245 hrs. 2nd Class Exam.Work.) Sgt Smith.
) Sgt Patterson.

Monday till Saturday. 1145-1245 hrs. 3rd Class Exam Work.) Lt Murray.
) Lt Whiteside.
) Sgt Taylor
) Sgt Holden.

(Sgnd.) Percy Fryer Lieut.
Battalion Education Officer.

12-9-19

Burgermeister,
MENDEN.

12th September, 1919.

In the name of the Burgermeisterie of Menden, I thank you for the assistance rendered by your fire-picquet to-day at Obermenden.

(Sgd) Lichtenberg,
Burgermeister.

J(a)

The Burgermeister,
 Menden.

Lieut. Colonel H.F. Watson, C.M.G., D.S.O., wishes to thank the Burgermeister of Menden for his letter dated 12th September, 1919, and is glad to know that his men were able to be of assistance.

(Sgd) G.F.Henson, 2/Lieut.
Asst. Adjt.,

51st Bn. The Manchester Regiment.

Menden.
13/9/19.

51st Bn Manchester Regiment.
===============================

TRAINING PROGRAMME FOR WEEK ENDING 27-9-19

DATE.	TIME.	NATURE OF TRAINING	PLACE.
22-9-19	0630-0730	Adjts Parade Drill	Menden *2nd & 3rd class Army Education*
	0930-1000	C.Os Parade "	" *Evans*
	1000-1130	Lecture on Scouting, passing of messages and reports, explanation of demonstration 23-9-19.	" (under Capt W...
23-9-19		*Casuals HQ. A & D Coys G.M.C.*	
	0630-0730	R.S.M.Parade Saluting Drill.	Menden
	0930-1130	Route March under Capt Walker and demonstration of lecture given 22-9-19	"
24-9-19	0630-0730	Adjts Parade Drill	"
		Brigade Sports.	Henneff
25-9-19		Rhine Trip.	
		Casuals HQ. A & D Coys GMC.	
26-9-19	0630-0730	Adjts Parade Drill	Menden
	0930-1000	C.Os Parade "	"
	1000-1130	L.G.Instruction under Lt O.Hamilton.	"
27-9-19	0630-0730	R.S.M.Parade Drill	"
	0930-1000	C.Os Parade "	"
	1000-1130	L.G.Instruction under Lt O.Hamilton	

Transport Officer will arrange to ... train his men in Driving and Riding.

Education each day at 1130 hrs.

Baths Monday and Tuesdays.

M.Os.Inspection.   Friday.

(Sgnd) T.F.Watson. Lieut Col.
Comdg. 51st Bn Manchester Regiment.

1st Bn Manchester Regiment.

PROGRAMME OF EDUCATION FOR WEEK ENDING SEPTEMBER 27th 1919

DAY	TIME	COY	SUBJECT	INSTRUCTOR
Monday	11.45-12.45	All Coys	2nd Class Certificate Exam	
	11.45-12.45	" "	3rd Class "	"
Tuesday	11.45-12.45	A	Arithmetic	Lieut Murray
	" "	A&B	"C" Group Arithmetic	Sgt Holden
	" "	"	Arithmetic	Sgt Smith
	" "	C&D	"C" Group	Pte Clarke
	" "	C	Arithmetic	Sgt Patterson
	" "	D	do	Sgt Taylor
Wednesday	11.45-12.45	A	English	Lt Murray
	" "	A&B	"C" Group English	Sgt Holden
	" "	B	English	Sgt Smith
	" "	C&D	"C" Group English	Pte Clarke
	" "	C	English	Sgt Patterson
	" "	D	do	Sgt Taylor
Thursday	11.45-12.45	A&B	Citizenship	Lt Fryer
	" "	C&D	"C" Group Arithmetic	Pte Clarke
	" "	C	Arithmetic	Sgt Patterson
	" "	D	do	Sgt Taylor
Friday	11.45-12.45	A	English	Lt Murray
	" "	A&B	"C" Group English	Sgt Holden
	" "	B	English	Sgt Smith
	" "	C&D	"C" Group English	Pte Clarke
	" "	C	English	Sgt Patterson
	" "	D	do	Sgt Taylor
Saturday	11.45-12.45	A	Arithmetic	Lt Murray
	" "	A&B	"C" Group Arithmetic	Sgt Holden
	" "	B	Arithmetic.	Sgt Smith
	" "	C&D	Citizenship	Lt Fryer

(Sgnd) P.Fryer Lieut.
Bn Education Officer

51st Bn Manchester Regiment.

SPORTS PROGRAMME FOR WEEK ENDING 28-9-19

DATE.	COY.	TIME.	PLACE	NATURE OF SPORT
22-9-19	No.13 Pltn 51st Mancs V Pltn 52nd Mncs Regt	1700	Menden	Boxing Final Bde Pltn Sports Cup.
23-9-19	A. Coy V. R.A.M.C.	1430	"	Football
24-9-19	Brigade Sports	1430	Henneff	
25-9-19	51st Manchesters		Rhine Trip.	
26-9-19	51st Mncs Reg V 51st Kings or Field Coy R.E.	1430	Menden	Football
27-9-19	No.4 Pltn V. No.8 Pltn.	1430	Menden	Soccer.

(Sgnd) G.S. Thwaites.
Bn Sports Officer.

RE-ORGANIZATION.

Owing to the shortage of men in the Battalion, it has been decided to reduce it by two companies.

Letter "D" Coy. will be amalgamated with letter "A" Coy. under the command of Captain C. D. Walker. Letter "C" Coy. will be amalgamated with "B" Company under the command of Lieut. J. Fox, M.C.

"Headquarters" Coy. under 2/Lieut. G. C. P. Grennan.

All available N.C.Os from "D" and "C" Companies will be transferred to "A" and "B" respectively for duty on Sunday, 21st inst., after Church Parade. They will take with them a transfer statement of clothing and equipment on A.F.W.3068.

They will take over the billets of these Coys. and will be paid and rationed by O.C. "A" and "B" Coys. respectively from on 1st October, 1919.

A cadre of "D" and "C" Coys. consisting of C.Q.M.S., clerk, storeman, and men due for demobilization will remain with "D" and "C" Coys. until the men have been demobilized and all the accounts and equipment and clothing ledgers are settled. This cadre will, however, be borne on the strength of their new Companies as from October 1st 1919 for rations and pay.

All surplus Lewis Guns, stores, etc., belonging to "D" and "C" Coys. will be handed over to the Quartermaster.

When the transfers are completed all Company records and books of "D" and "C" Coys. will be handed into the Orderly Room.

Certificates will be handed in by O.C. Coys. when the accounts are finally closed that all is correct and that there are no deficiencies.

Conduct sheets (A.F. B.122) will be transferred with the men. O.C. Coys. will render a certificate when the transfers are completed that they are in possession of A.F. B.122 for every N.C.O. and man in their Company.

Major H. Wood, M.C. will take over P.R.I. and Battalion Messing arrangements.

2/Lieut. G.C.P.Grennan will, in addition to his duties as O.C. "H.Q" Coy. train the scouts of the Battalion.

The following is the detail of Officers on amalgamation. They will report for duty to their new Company Commanders after Church Parade on Sunday, 21st inst.

P.R.I. & Officer i/c Messing Headquarters.	Major H. Wood, M.C.
	Capt. G. Twigg, Adjt.
	2/Lieut. G. F. Henson, Assist. Adjt.
Civil Administrator	Lieut. H. L. Willoughby,
Sports Officer	Lieut. G. S. Thwaits.
Quartermaster.	Capt. D. Smith.
Asst. Q.M.	Lieut. H. E. Thornton, M.C.
Signal Officer	2/Lieut. A. Heaton.
Lewis Gun Officer	Lieut. O. Hamilton.
Education Officers.	Lieut. P. Fryer
	Lieut. D. Whiteside.
	Lieut. R. W. Murray.
Transport Officer	Lieut. F. C. Gower.
"A" Company. Officer Commanding.	Capt. C. D. Walker.
2-in-C.	Lieut. J.L.Galloway.
	Lieut. S.E.Gwinnell.
	Lieut. G. Hunt.
	Lieut. C.H.Hansard.
	Lieut. J. Peregrine.
	Lieut. P.E.A.Kent.
	2/Lieut. P. Ryan.
	2/Lieut. W.J.Lockie.
"B" Company. Officer Commanding.	Lieut. J. Fox, M.C.
2-in-C.	Lieut. H.E.Humphrey-Moore.
	2/Lieut. A. Collens, D.C.M.
	2/Lieut. E. Aitken-Davies.
	2/Lieut. F. C. Taylor.
	2/Lieut. R. N. Bates.
	2/Lieut. H. Hetherington.

RE-ORGANIZATION (continued).

The following N.C.Os are detailed to take over various appointments at Headquarters as shown against their names:

Quartermaster Sgt.	R.Q.M.S. Barnes.
R Sgt's Clerk.	Pte. Collister vice =/c Stoddard.
Orderly Sgt / Room Sgt	Col.Sgt. Warburton.
Sgt. Drummer.	Corpl. ~~Kxxxxxxx~~ Pearson.
Provost Sgt.	Sgt. Prince.
Scouts Sgt.	Cpl. Wagstaffe. (To be recalled Bde. School).
	L/c. Hollis. "D" Coy.
Scout Cpl.	Sgt. Cawston.
Signal Sgt.	
Sgt. Instructors.	Sgt. Maxwell to assist C.S.M. Such
Musketry.	Col. Hindo.
P. & B.T.	Cpl. Mills.
Lewis Gun.	Nil.
Bombing	L/c. Bowers.
Gas.	~~L/c. Butterworth~~. Pte. Quinn.
Pioneer Sgt.	Sgt. Davies.
Sgt. Cook.	L/c. Mellor.
Transport.	L/c. Woodruff.
Water Duties.	L/c. Maddox.
Sanitary.	Pte. Aldcroft (Senior man).
Sgt. Tailor.	Pte. Chambers (Senior man).
Shoemaker.	

In cases where no N.C.O. has been detailed or there is a shortage of the establishment the Adjutant must be at once informed with a view to filling up the deficiencies.

"A" & "D" Coys.	C.S.M.	C.S.M. Morris.
	C.Q.M.S.	C.Q.M.S. Browne
"B" & "C" Coys.	C.S.M.	C.S.M. Morgan.
	C.Q.M.S.	C.Q.M.S. Clegg.

H Watson Lieut. Col. Comdg.,
1st Bn. The Manchester Regiment.

ORDERS IN THE EVENT OF A DISTURBANCE IN THE AREA.

The Battalion consists to two Companies A & B, and Headquarters Coy.
The Battalion is located in billets, A Coy and H.Q. towards the South end of the village on the Meindorf Road. B Coy. is located in billets towards the West end of the town on the Siegburg-Mulldorf Road.
On the alarm being sounded the Coys. will at once fall in on their Company parade ground; H.Q. Coy. will fall in at the Q.M. Stores, and with the Quarter Guard will take charge of the stores and ammunition.
"A" Coy. will send one platoon to guard the Battalion Signal Office. One platoon to remain at their Coy. Headquarters to guard stores and Battalion workshops. The remaining two platoons under O.C. Coy. will proceed to Battalion Orderly Room and await instructions.
"B" Coy. will fall-in on their Coy. parade ground and O.C. Coy. will detail one platoon as guard to stores, etc. The remainder under O.C. Coy. will move to the school square opposite the Officers' Mess. O.C. Coys. after having taken up their positions will send ammunition parties to draw sufficient ammunition to make up each man to 100 rounds.
The Transport Section will fall in at their Horse Lines and await further orders.
Officers in charge of Coys. or platoons will not interfere with any civil disturbance if the civil authorities can handle the situation themselves and provided no British Troops are implicated. If, however, there is a likelihood of damage being done to property belonging to the British Government or German property in use by British Troops; if British Troops are implicated or if civil authorities cannot cope with the situation the officers on the spot must take whatever action they consider necessary.
In the event of a Platoon or Company being sent to an adjoining town to assist in keeping the peace the officer commanding the platoon or Company will place himself and his men at the disposal of the A.P.M. or whoever has asked for the assistance of the Troops.

Lieut. Col. Commanding
 1st Bn. The Manchester Regiment.

51st Bn Manchester Regiment.

REVISED EDUCATION PROGRAMME FOR WEEKENDING SEPTEMBER 27th 1919

DAY.	TIME.	COY.	SUBJECT.	INSTRUCTOR.
Tue.	11.45-12.45	A	Arithmetic	Lt Murray
	"	"	"C" Group Arithmetic	Sgt Holden
	"	B	Arithmetic	Sgt Smith
	"	"	"C" Group Arithmetic	Sgt Patterson
Wed.	"	A	Geography	Sgt Taylor
	"	"	"C" Group Geography	Sgt Holden
	"	B	History.	Sgt Smith
	"	"	"C" Group History	Sgt Patterson
Thu.	"	A	History	Sgt Smith
	"	"	"C" Group History	Sgt Patterson
	"	B	Geography	Sgt Taylor
	"	"	"C" Group Geography	Sgt Holden
Fri.	"	A	English	Lt Murray
	"	"	"C" Group English	Sgt Holden
	"	B	English	Sgt Smith
	"	"	"C" Group English	Sgt Patterson
Sat.	"	A&B	Citizenship	Lt Fryer

(Sgnd) ?.Fryer Lieut.
Bn Education Officer.

51st Bn Manchester Regiment.

SPORTS PROGRAMME FOR WEEK ENDING OCTOBER 5th 1919

DATE.	COY.	TIME.	PLACE	NATURE OF SPORT
28-9-19	51st Manos V. 51st Kings.	1430	Hondon	Football
29-9-19	Battalion	"	"	Rugby Practice
30-9-19	Brigade	"	"	Horse Show
	51st Manos V. R.E.	"	"	Soccer
1-10-19	Officers V. Sergts.	"	"	Soccer
2-10-19	A.Coy V. B.Coy.	"	"	Soccer
3-10-19	Battalion	"	"	Rugby Practice
4-10-19	H.Q.Coy V. Winners			
	A.Coy V. B.Coy.	"	"	Soccer
5-10-19 x	51st Manos Regt V. 52nd Kings Regt	"	"	Soccer

x This match not certain.

27-9-19

(Sgnd) G.S. Thwaite Lieut.
Bn Sports Officer.

51st BN. THE MANCHESTER REGIMENT.

PROGRAMME OF EDUCATIONAL TRAINING FOR WEEK ENDING OCT. 4th 1919.

Day.	Time.	Coy.	Subject.	Instructor.
Mon.	1145-1245	"A"	Arithmetic.	Lieut. Murray.
"	"	A "C" Group.	"	Sergt. Holden.
"	"	"B"	"	" Smith.
"	"	B "C" Group.	"	" Paterson.
Tue.	"	"A"	Geography.	Sergt. Taylor.
"	"	A "C" Group.	"	" Holden.
"	"	"B"	History.	" Smith.
"	"	B "C" Group.	"	" Paterson.
Wed.	"	"A"	English.	Lieut. Murray.
"	"	A "C" Group.	"	Sergt. Holden.
"	"	"B"	"	" Smith.
"	"	B "C" Group.	"	" Paterson.
Thu.	"	"A"	History.	Sergt. Smith.
"	"	A "C" Group.	"	" Paterson.
"	"	"B"	Geography.	Lieut. Murray.
"	"	B "C" Group.	"	Sergt. Taylor.
Fri.	"	"A"	Gen. Knowledge.	Lieut. Murray.
"	"	A "C" Group.	" "	Sergt. Holden.
"	"	"B"	" "	" Taylor.
"	"	B "C" Group.	" "	" Paterson.
Sat.	"	" A & B.	Citizenship.	Lieut. Fryer.

EDEN.
23rd September, 1919.

(Sgd) Percy Fryer, Lieut.
Education Officer,
51st Bn. The Manchester Regt.

WAR DIARY or INTELLIGENCE SUMMARY

Army Form C. 2118.

Place	Date	Hour	Summary of Events and Information	Remarks and references to Appendices
MENDEN	1/10/19		Cadres of B Coy & HQ Coy from GMC - Remainder having usual programme - 2/Lt Chandler reported as reporting Battalion	
	2/10/19		Cadres of B Coy finish GMC. H&Q Coy also firing - Visit of DDMS. Inspector of Villa, sanitary arrangements etc - Rugby football match v 51st King's Liverpool Regt.	
	3/10/19		Range not in use owing to bad weather conditions - No 85964 Sgt Jones NE found "not guilty" by FGCM - Medical Inspection Training. Sports Education programme for week Ending 11th inst drawn up. 156 Brigade Boxing Tournament at HENNEF Result - this Battalion represented in finals the finals at each weight.	A B C
	4/10/19		HQ Coy on Range complete less II GMC - Battalion Transport moved from their accommodation and are now located at TAUNHOL FARM Vehicles parked in Triangle field at Farm - Football HQrs v A Coy	
	5/10/19		Church parade - Drafts for Brigade Horse Show - Football Battalion team v 51st King's (Liverpool) Regt - Caps & NCOs Lecture	

Relieved from leave to UK.

Army Form C. 2118.

WAR DIARY
or
INTELLIGENCE SUMMARY.
(Erase heading not required.)

Instructions regarding War Diaries and Intelligence Summaries are contained in F. S. Regs., Part II. and the Staff Manual respectively. Title pages will be prepared in manuscript.

Place	Date	Hour	Summary of Events and Information	Remarks and references to Appendices
11/F/NDRN	6/10/19		Arrivals of HQ, A + B Coys. firing of MG, fitting of clothing, stores of QM, and stannels, purchase of "A" Coy. — Bathing, Transport and "A" Coy — Brigade Boxing Tournament at HENNEF — thanks this Battalion games to join, and 2 second prizes — Additional prize (silver cup) for most meritorious and cleanest horses won by Sgt Hope of this Battalion	
	7/10/19		Arrivals of HQ, A + B Coys. firing GMC (part III) — Remington platoons at tallinwn "B" Coy. HQ, Transport — Bathing HQ + B Coys also events and basket yesterday — Three battalion players selected for Divisional Rugby team v. X" Corps at BONN — Battalion football trial for selection of Soccer Team — Concert in Recreation Room given by Sergeants Mess.	
	8/10/19		Arrivals of HQ, A + B Coys completes Part III GMC — Remington training open programme — Rugby football A v "B" Coys.	
	9/10/19		Training as per programme — Lieut Hutchence returned from leave to U.K.	

Army Form C. 2118.

WAR DIARY
or
INTELLIGENCE SUMMARY.
(Erase heading not required.)

Instructions regarding War Diaries and Intelligence Summaries are contained in F. S. Regs., Part II. and the Staff Manual respectively. Title pages will be prepared in manuscript.

Place	Date	Hour	Summary of Events and Information	Remarks and references to Appendices
MENDEN	10/10/19		Training as per programme — Medical Inspection — Brigade Horse Show Polo Semi finals, Battalion team qualify for final — Football v 53rd Battn. Gunner - Sergeant reported for duty in battalion — Gunnery, Sports & Education programme for week ending 18th October App. Lieut. P.S.C. Hunt reported from course at Keble College, Oxford. 2/Lt J.R. Peigrue reported on discharge from Hospital.	(D) E F
	11/10/19		Brigade Horse Show — 4 firsts, 5 seconds, 3 thirds in Battalion Competitors. 3 O.R's sent to COVERNT for demobilisation.	
	12/10/19		Church Parade — 8 O.R's sent to COVERNT for demobilisation	
	13/10/19		All available escorts on range for G.M.C. Remainder training as per programme — 9 O.R's sent to COVERNT for demobilisation. Battery - A Coy Transport. Football Semi Final Corps Cross Competition Results 84th R.G.A 6, 5" Batt. 2 — leave to 4th regiment —	
	14/10/19		Escorts complete part III — Remainder training as per programme	

Army Form C. 2118.

WAR DIARY
or
INTELLIGENCE SUMMARY.
(Erase heading not required.)

Instructions regarding War Diaries and Intelligence Summaries are contained in F. S. Regs., Part II. and the Staff Manual respectively. Title pages will be prepared in manuscript.

Place	Date	Hour	Summary of Events and Information	Remarks and references to Appendices
MENDEN	4/1/19		Bathing — HQ Coy "B" transferred not marked yesterday — 7 O.R.s proceeded to CONZENT for demobilization — Guard mounted at Brigade HdQrs —	
	5/1/19		Church — G.M.C. — Remainder of Battalion route march. Instruction in use of maps, compass & field glasses — four inspections — 2/Lt G.C.P. GERNAN returned from 47th Gen. Hospital	
	16/0/19		Church — G.M.C. — Remainder L.G. training & gun programme — 9 O.R.s proceeded to CONZENT — Major G. Denkin D.S.O. & remainder of G.C.M. assembling in BONN today — Commanding Officers at Brigade Commanders Conference at Brigade HQ., ref Rugby Football amalgamation and reorganisation — Corps Rugby Football competition — this Battalion beat 13th Kings — Concert at HENNEF and presentation of prizes for boxing & shows staged —	
	7/1/19		Church — G.M.C. — Remainder L.G. firing on Range — 2 O.R.s	

D. D. & L., London, E.C.
(A8001) Wt. W.1771/M2931 750,000 5/17 Sch. 52 Forms/C2.1.0/14

Army Form C. 2118.

WAR DIARY
or
INTELLIGENCE SUMMARY.
(Erase heading not required.)

Instructions regarding War Diaries and Intelligence Summaries are contained in F. S. Regs., Part II. and the Staff Manual respectively. Title pages will be prepared in manuscript.

Place	Date	Hour	Summary of Events and Information	Remarks and references to Appendices
MENDEN	17/10/19		Proceeded to CONCERT also Capt & QM-D. Smith – Medical Inspection – Training, Sports, Education programmes WE 257/10/19 – Whist drive in "B" Coy dining Hall –	G H I
	18/10/19		Cinemato funny GMC – Remainder L.G. firing on Range – August Silent Party in "B" Coy dining Hall –	
	19/10/19		Church Parade – Men returning from leave to UK, medically inspected, bathed and clothing changed before rejoining Coy – Football – Officers v WO's & Sergeants pBath.	
	20/10/19		Cinemato continue GMC including men returned from leave – Orders received and never that the battalion is being retained for the present with Army of the Rhine – will be formed into companies – the depots to be transferred to 52nd Lancashire Battery "A" Coy Transport – Rugby football – Officers v WO's & Sgts.	
	21/10/19		Cinemato GMC – Remainder having as per programme –	

Army Form C. 2118.

WAR DIARY
or
INTELLIGENCE SUMMARY.
(Erase heading not required.)

Instructions regarding War Diaries and Intelligence Summaries are contained in F. S. Regs., Part II. and the Staff Manual respectively. Title pages will be prepared in manuscript.

Place	Date	Hour	Summary of Events and Information	Remarks and references to Appendices
MENDEN	21/10/19		5 O.Rs. proceeded to CONTENT for demobilisation — Owing to reorganisation & transfers, all leave vacancies for 22nd November, later have been retained — Bathing. B Coy HQ + recruits — Commanding officers attended Brigade Commanders Conference reference amalgamation + reorganisation of Battalion. Details of 53rd Bn, are to be transferred to this Battalion and transfers completed by 24th inst.	
	22/10/19		Brigade Horse Show (1 jump prize) Lieut GALLOWAY and party proceeded to FEUERWERKE LABORATORIUM (near SIEGBURG) as the Equipment found on arrival there — Practise on Competition for G.M.C. Cup (Highest Coy average for Part III) "A" Coy winner of Cup + 86.105 Sgt Carleton winner of medal for highest total for Part III (Score 135 pts) Results :—	
			A Coy Total average 76.07	
			B " " " 64.26	
			C " " " 73.57	
			D " " " 69.97	

Army Form C. 2118.

WAR DIARY
or
INTELLIGENCE SUMMARY.
(Erase heading not required.)

Instructions regarding War Diaries and Intelligence Summaries are contained in F.S. Regs., Part II. and the Staff Manual respectively. Title pages will be prepared in manuscript.

Place	Date	Hour	Summary of Events and Information	Remarks and references to Appendices
MENDEN	22/10/19		Prizes also awarded for the two first results in each Coy.	
	23/10/19		Corporals GMC. Commanding Officer proceeded on special leave (4 days) to U.K. — 2 Officers volunteered for transfer to 52nd Bn. Rugby Football Semi-Final Corps Championship 51st Bn. 14, KIVk. 3 goals	
	24/10/19		Corporals GMC. Barometer Route March — 17.0.72. (Transferred from 53rd Bn.) reported on arrival — Lieut F.C. Taylor returned from leave to U.K. Training, Sports & Education programme for week ending 2nd November 1919	J K L App
	25/10/19		Corporals GMC. — Eleven mounted at Bergall Headquarters. Lieut R.W. Murray and F.C. Taylor proceeded to CONGENT for 2/Lieut G.C.P. Brennan proceeded to 52nd Bn. (Transferred) demobilisation — 9 Officers (from 53rd Bn.) under return of amalgamation — 9 Officers taken on strength 151st Bn from today also Capt Williams C.F. Lieut Cottley M.C. (att. Bde HQ) and Mr R. Stephenson (L.T.M. Bty)	

WAR DIARY or INTELLIGENCE SUMMARY.

Army Form C. 2118.

(Erase heading not required.)

Place	Date	Hour	Summary of Events and Information	Remarks and references to Appendices
MENDEN	26/10/19		Church Parade – Medical Inspection – 5 O/Rs proceeded to England for demobilisation –	
	27/10/19		No firing owing to bad weather – Rugby Final Corps Competition Vienna X Corps Troops. Results 9pts down after extra time. Replay on Thursday –	
	28/10/19		Ceased firing 6MC – Remainder training as per programme – Bathing under Company arrangements as Baths at FRIEDRICH-WILHELMS HOTÉ are out of order – 2/Lts Dimple and Stephenson proceeded to ENGENT for demobilisation –	
	29/10/19		Ceased 6MC – Remainder Route March – instruction in Empire Works, map reading. Practice alarm for return in case of civilian disturbance. Lt-Col Watson CMG, DSO, returning from special leave to UK. Hear he is posted to 52nd Battalion with effect from 25-10-19. Lieut Galloway reported on return from Battalion Equipment Exam –	

Army Form C. 2118.

WAR DIARY
or
INTELLIGENCE SUMMARY.
(Erase heading not required.)

Instructions regarding War Diaries and Intelligence Summaries are contained in F. S. Regs., Part II. and the Staff Manual respectively. Title pages will be prepared in manuscript.

Place	Date	Hour	Summary of Events and Information	Remarks and references to Appendices
MENDEN	29/10/19		Major A.K.D. Lillard (late 53rd Bn) struck off the strength of the Battalion on proceeding to England to rejoin Regular Battalion.	
	30/10/19		Coronel G.M.C. Remainder Training as per programme – Football Replayed Final Rugby & Cup Competition at BONN. 51st Battalion winners. 6 O.R. Proceeded to CONCERT Given as per programme – Lieut E.S. Thwaits proceeded to COBLENZ as competitor for American Boxing Tournament. Medical Inspection – 1 O.R. proceeded to CONCERT for ambulance.	
	31/10/19		247. Wethering returned to Battalion on termination of course at Commercial College, COLOGNE.	

J Watson
Lieut. Colonel
Commanding 51st Bn. Manchester Regt.

51st Bn Manchester Regiment.
===================================

TRAINING PROGRAMME FOR WEEK ENDING 4th OCTOBER 1919

MONDAY.

0630-0730	Adjts Parade Drill	London
0930-1015	C.Os Parade "	"
1015-1130	Platoon Drill & Guard Drill	
	Casuals Firing G.M.C.	Range.

TUESDAY.

0630-0730	R.S.M.Parade Saluting.	London
0930-1015	C.Os Parade Drill	"
1015-1130	Platoon & Guard Drill	
	Casuals Firing G.M.C.	"

WEDNESDAY.

0630-0730	Adjts Parade Drill	London
0930-1015	C.Os Parade "	"
1015-1130	Lecture on Scouting,sending of	
	messages and reports, explanation	
	of scheme 2-10-19 (under senior officer)	
	Casuals Firing G.M.C.	

THURSDAY.

0630-0730	R.S.M.Parade. Drill.	London
0930-1130	Route March & demonstrative	"
	of lecture given 1-10-19	"
	Casuals Firing G.M.C.	

FRIDAY.

0630-0730	Adjts Parade Drill.	London
0930-1000	C.Os Parade "	"
1000-1045	Bombing.	"
1045-1130	Gas	"
	Casuals Firing G.M.C.	"

SATURDAY.

0630-0730	R.S.M.Parade Drill	London
0930-1015	C.Os Parade "	"
1015-1130	L.G.Instruction under	
	Lt Hamilton.	"
	Casuals Firing G.M.C.	

Transport Officer will train his men in Driving and Riding
Education each day 1130hrs.
Baths   Monday & Tuesday.
M.O.Inspection. Thursday.

(Sgnd) H.F.Watson   Lieut Col
Comdg 51st Bn Manchester Regiment

51st Bn Manchester Regiment.
===================================

TRAINING PROGRAMME FOR WEEK ENDING OCTOBER 12th 1919

MONDAY.

0900-1000	C.Os.Parade.	Battalion Parade Ground
1000-1100	Extended order Drill.	"	"	"
1100-1200	P.T. under Cpl.Hind.	"	"	"
	Casuals Firing G.M.C.	"	"	"

TUESDAY.

0900-1000	C.Os.Parade.	"	"	"
1000-1030	Guard Drill.	"	"	"
1030-1100	Saluting Drill	"	"	"
1100-1200	Bombing & L.G. under Lt Hamilton.
	Casuals Firing G.M.C.

WEDNESDAY.

0900-1000	C.Os.Parade.	"	"	"
1000-1100	Extended order Drill	"	"	"
1100-1200	Section & Pltn Drill	"	"	"
	Casuals Firing G.M.C.	"	"	"

THURSDAY.

0900-1230	Route March.	"	"	"
1400	Feet Inspection.	"	"	"

FRIDAY.

0900-1000	C.Os.Parade.	"	"	"
1000-1100	Method of advancing under Fire.
	Section 158 of I.T. 1914 Lecture & Demonstration.
1100-1200	Arms Drill 1/2 hr. Guard Drill 1/2 hr.
	Casuals Firing G.M.C.

SATURDAY.

0900-1000	C.Os.Parade	"	"	"
1000-1100	Lecture & Demonstration on Outpost
	Patrols Sect.158 I.T.	"	"	"
1100-1130	Saluting under R.S.M.	"	"	"
1130-1200	Gas Drill.	"	"	"
	Casuals Firing G.M.C.

NOTE.

Transport Officer will arrange to train his men in Riding &
                                                                                           Driving.

Baths. Monday & Tuesday Afternoon.
M.O.Inspection. Thursday.
Changeing Clothing Friday.

3-10-19

                                                      (Sgnd) H.F.Watson. LT.Col,Comdg
                                                      51st Bn Manchester Regiment

51st Bn. Manchester Regiment.

SPORTS PROGRAMME FOR WEEK ENDING OCTOBER 12th 1919

DATE.	COY.	TIME.	PLACE.	NATURE OF SPORT.
5-10-19	51st Mancs. V. 51st Kings.	1430	Menden	Soccer.
6-10-19	Brigade Boxing (Final)	1730	Hennoff	Boxing
7-10-19	Battalion (A) V Rest Bn.(B)	1430	Menden	Football.
8-10-19	Rugby Practice		Menden	Rugby.
9-10-19	"A" Coy V. "B" Coy.	1430	Menden	Soccer
10-10-19	"H.Q." Coy V. winners "A" V. "B" Coy.	1430	Menden	Soccer
11-10-19	Brigade Horse Show	-	Hennoff	-
12-10-19	Battalion	1430	Menden	Soccer.

(Sgnd) O. Hamilton, Lieut.
For Bn. Sports Officer.

51st. BN. THE MANCHESTER REGT.

PROGRAMME OF EDUCATIONAL TRAINING FOR WEEK ENDING 11th. OCTOBER 19

Day.	Time.	Coy.	Subject.	Instructor.	
Monday.	1145--1245.	"A"	Arithmetic.	Lieut.	Murray.
"	"	"A"c group.	"	Sergt.	Holden.
"	"	"B"	"	"	Smith.
"	"	"B"c group.	"	"	Paterson.
Tuesday.	"	"	"A"	Geography.	"	Taylor.
"	"	"	"B"	History.	"	Smith.
"	"	"	"A"c group.	Geography.	"	Holden.
"	"	"	"B"c group.	History.	"	Paterson.
Wednesday.	"	"	"A"	English.	Lieut.	Murray.
"	"	"	"A"c group.	"	Sergt.	Holden.
"	"	"	"B"	"	"	Smith.
"	"	"	"B"c group.	"	"	Paterson.
Thursday.	"	"	"A"	History.	"	Smith.
"	"	"	"A"c group.	"	"	Paterson.
"	"	"	"B"	Geography.	Lieut.	Murray.
"	"	"	"B"c group.	"	Sergt.	Taylor.
Friday.	"	"	"A"	Gen. Knöledge	Lieut.	Murray.
"	"	"	"A"c group.	" "	Sergt.	Holden.
"	"	"	"B"c group.	" "	"	Taylor.
"	"	"	"B"	" "	"	Paterson.
Saturday.	"	"	"A & B"	Citizenship.	Lieut.	Fryer.

INDEN.
10-1919.

(Sgd.) PERCY FRYER, Lieut.
Education Officer,
51st. Bn, The Manchester Regiment.

51st Bn Manchester Regt.

TRAINING PROGRAMME FOR WEEK ENDING OCTOBER 18t 1919

MONDAY.

0900-0930	C.Os.Inspection.	Bn Parade Ground.
0930-1100	Lewis Gun Class Lt Hamilton & Sgt Mills	
1100-1130	Lecture on Bombing	

TUESDAY.

0900-0930	C.Os.Inspection.	Bn Parade Ground
0930-1145	Lewis Gun Class Lt Hamilton & Sgt Mills	

WEDNESDAY.

0900-0930	C.Os Inspection	Bn Parade Ground
0930-1145	~~Lewis Gun Class Lt Hamilton & Sgt Mills~~	

[handwritten: Route march. Instruction in maps. Compasses & foot inspection]

THURSDAY.

0900-1145	Lewis Gun Firing on Range under Lt Hamilton.

FRIDAY.

0900-1145	Lewis Gun Firing on range under Lt Hamilton.

SATURDAY.

0900-1145	Lewis Gun Firing on range under Lt Hamilton.

NOTES

1. Baths. - Monday & Tuesday afternoon.
2. M.Os. Inspection - Thursday afternoon
3. Changing Clothing - Friday afternoon.
4. Transport Class Daily - Riding and Driving under Lt Gower
5. Education 1145-1245 hrs daily.

10-10-19   (Sgnd) H.F.Watson Lieut Col.
            Comdg. 51st Bn Manchester Regiment

51st Bn Manchester Regiment.

SPORTS PROGRAMME FOR WEEK ENDING OCTOBER 19th 1919

DATE	COY.	TIME	PLACE	NATURE OF SPORT
13-10-19	51st Mancs Reg. V Winners 5th Borders V 52nd Kings.	1430	Hofgarten Bonn	Soccer Div. Knock out Comp
14-10-19	Transport V No.4 Pltn.	1430	Menden	Soccer
15-10-19	Drummers V. H.Q. Coy.	1430	Menden	Soccer
"	Rugby Practice	1800	"	Rugby
16-10-19	51st Mancs Reg. V. 13th Kings	1500	"	"
17-10-19	Battalion.	1830	"	Dance
18-10-19	51st Mancs V. 51st Kings.	1400	"	Athletic Comp and Cross Country Ra
19-10-19	Battalion.	1430	"	Soccer Practic
20-10-19) 21-10-19)	51st. Manchester Regt. V. 52nd. Manchester Regt. *KINGS.*		Obercassel.	Competition in Musketry, Rugby, Soccer & X Country

10-10-19.

(Signed) G. S. THWAITS, Lt.
Sports Officer,
51st. Bn. the Manchester Regt.

51st Bn Manchester Regiment

PROGRAMME OF EDUCATION FOR W/E OCTOBER 18th 1919

DAY.	TIME.	COY.	SUBJECT.		INSTRUCTOR.
Mon.	11.45-12.45	A	Arithmetic		Lieut Murray.
"	"	"	do	"C" Group	Sergt Holden.
"	"	B	do		Sergt Smith
"	"	"	do	"C" Group	Sergt Patterson
Tue	"	A	Geogbaphy		Sergt Taylor
"	"	"	do	"C" Group	Sergt Holden
"	"	B	History.		Sergt Smith
"	"	"	do	"C" Group	Sergt Patterson.
Wed	"	A	English		Lieut Murray.
"	"	"	do	"C" Group	Sergt Holden
"	"	B	do		Sergt Smith
"	"	"	do	"C" Group	Sergt Patterson.
Thur.	"	A	History		Sergt Smith
"	"	"	do	"C" Group	Sergt Patterson
"	"	B	Geography		Lieut Murray.
"	"	"	do	"C" Group	Sergt Taylor
Fri.	"	A	Gen.Knowledge		Lieut Murray.
"	"	"	do	"C" Group	Sergt Holden.
"	"	B	do		Sergt Taylor
"	"	"	do	"C" Group	Sergt Patterson.
Sat.	"	A	Citizenship.		Lieut Fryer
"	"	"	do	"C" Group	do
"	"	B	do		do
"	"	"	do	"C" Group	do

10-10-19

(Sgnd) P.Fryer Lieut
Bn Education Officer

51st Bn Manchester Regiment.

PROGRAMME OF TRAINING FOR WEEK ENDING OCTOBER 25th 1919

MONDAY.

0900-0930	C.Os.Parade.	Bn Parade Ground.
0930-1030	Lecture & Illustration on No.5 Mills Grenade.	
1030-1130	Practice Fusing and Cleaning Bombs.	

TUESDAY.

0900-0930	C.Os.Parade.	Bn Parade Ground
0930-1030	Lewis Gunning.	
1030-1130	do do	

WEDNESDAY.

0900-1230	Battalion Route March.

THURSDAY.

0900-0930	C.Os.Parade.	Bn Parade Ground.
0930-1030	Throwing Dummy Bombs from Cage.	
1030-1130	Extended order work by squads.	

FRIDAY.

0900-0930	C.Os.Parade.	Bn Parade Ground
0930-1030	Lewis Gunning.	
1030-1130	do do	

SATURDAY.

0900-0930	C.Os.Parade	Bn Parade Ground.
0930-1000)	Lecture on 36 Bombs &	
1000-1130)	"Cup" Discharger . Live Bomb Throwing demonstrated by Instructor, followed by throwing by individuals under instruction.	

NOTES.

Education as per Eduction Programme.
Sports,   as per Sports   "
Bathing Mondays & Tuesdays.
Medical Inspection. Thursday.
Changeing Clothing Friday.

15-10-19   (Sgnd)   H F.Watson Lieut Col Comdg.,
                                       51st Bn Manchester Regiment.

51st Bn Manchester Regiment.
===============================

SPORTS PROGRAMME FOR WEEK ENDING 25-10-19

DATE.	OCY.	TIME.	PLACE.	NATURE OF SPORT
19-10-19	Officers V. Serjeants.	1430	Menden	Soccer.
20-10-19 & 21-10-19	51st Manchester Regt V. 2nd Kings L'pool Regt.		Born.	Competition in Musketry, Rugby, Soccer & Cross Country
22-10-19	A.Coy. V. B.Coy. (H.Q. to be includ. with Coys)	1430	Menden	Rugby.
24-10-19	Transport V. No.5 Pltn	1430	"	Soccer.
25-10-19	H.Q.Coy V. "B" Coy.	1430	"	Soccer.
25-10-19	No.2 Pltn.V.No.6 Pltn	1430	"	Soccer.

17-10-19

(Sgnd) G.S.Thwaite. Lieut.
Battalion Sports Officer.

51st. BN. THE MANCHESTER REGIMENT.

PROGAMME OF EDUCATIONAL TRAINING FOR WEEKENDING 25TH OCTOBER 1919.

Day.	Time.	Coy.	Subject.	Instructor.
Monday	1145-1245y	"A"	Arithmetic	Lieut. Murray.
"	" "	"A" c group	"	Sergt. Holden
"	" "	"B"	"	" Taylor
"	" "	"B" c group	"	" Paterson.
Tuesday	" "	"A"	Geography	" Taylor
"	" "	"A" c group	"	" Holden
"	" "	"B"	History	Lieut. Whiteside.
"	" "	"B" c group	"	Sergt Paterson,
Wednesday	" "	"A"	English	Lieut Murray
"	" "	"A" c group	"	Sergt Holden.
"	" "	"B"	"	Lieut Whiteside,
"	" "	"B" c group	"	Sergt Taylor
Thursday	" "	"A"	History	Lieut Whiteside
"	" "	"A" c group	"	Sergt Paterson
"	" "	"B"	Geography	Lieut Murray
"	" "	"B" c group	"	Sergt Taylor.
Friday	" "	"A"	Gen Knowledge	Lieut Murray
"	" "	"A" c group	" "	Sergt Holden
"	" "	"B"	" "	" Taylor
"	" "	"B" c group	" "	" Paterson
Saturday	" "	"A" & "B"	Citizenship	Lieut Fryer

RANDEN 16th October 1919.

(Sgd) PERCY FRYER, Lieut.
Education Officer,
51st. BN. THE MANCHESTER REGIMENT,

51st Bn Manchester Regiment.

TRAINING PROGRAMME FOR WEEK ENDING   1st NOVEMBER 1919

MONDAY.

Battalion.	0900-0930	C.Os.Parade.	Bn Parade Ground.
A.Coy.	0930-1130	Lewis Gunning.	
B.Coy.	0930-1130	Bombing.	

TUESDAY.

Battalion.	0900-0930	C.Os.Parade	Bn Parade Ground.
A.Comy	0930-1130	Bombing.	
B.Coy.	0930-1130	Lewis Gunning.	

WEDNESDAY.

Battalion.	0900-0930	Route March.

THURSDAY.

Battalion.	0900-0930	C.Os.Parade.	Bn Parade Ground.
A.Coy.	0930-1130	Lewis Gunning.	
B "	0930-1130	Bombing.	

FRIDAY.

Battalion	0900-0930	C.Os.Parade.	Bn Parade Ground.
A.Coy.	0930-1130	Bombing.	
B "	0930-1130	Lewis Gunning.	

SATURDAY.

Battalion.	0900-0930	C.Os.Parade.	Bn Parade Ground.
A.Coy.	0930-1130	Lewis Gunning.	
B.Coy.	0930-1130	Bombing.	

NOTES.

Owing to the large number of men returning from Leave during the last few days, the specalist programme for last week has had to be repeated.

24-10-19

(Sgnd)   G.Devlin. Major.
51st Bn Manchester Regiment

5?st Bn Manchester Regiment.

SPORTS PROGRAMME FOR WEEK ENDING 2nd NOVEMBER 1919

DATE.	COY.	TIME.	PLACE.	NATURE SPORT
27-10-19	No.2 Pltn. V. No.6 Pltn.	1430	Menden	Soccer
28-10-19	H.Q.Coy V. B.Coy.	1430	"	"
29-10-19	A.Coy V. B.Coy.	1430	"	Rugby
30-10-19	Officers V. Sergts.	1430	"	Soccer
31-10-19	Transport V. No.5 Pltn.	1430	"	
1-11-19	No.2 Pltn. V. No.6 Pltn.	1430	"	
2-11-19	Sergts V. Rest Battalion.	1430	"	

24-10-19

(Sgnd) G.S.Thwaites
Battalion Sports Officer

51st Bn Manchester Regiment.

PROGRAMME OF EDUCATIONAL TRAINING FOR WEEK ENDING NOV.1st 1919

DAY	TIME	GOY.	SUBJECT	INSTRUCTOR
Mon	1145-1245	A	Arithmetic.	Sergt Holder
"	"	" C Group	do	" "
"	"	B	do	Sergt Firth.
"	"	" C Group	do	" "
Tue.	1145-1245	A	Geography	Sergt Firth
"	"	" C Group	do	" Holder
"	"	B	do	Lieut Whiteside
"	"	" C Group	do	" "
Wed.	1145-1245	A	English.	Lieut Murray
"	"	" C Group	do	Sergt Holder
"	"	B	do	Lieut Whiteside
"	"	" C Group	do	Sergt Firth
Thu.	1145-1245	A	History.	Lieut Whiteside
"	"	" C Group	do	Lieut Whiteside
"	"	B	Geography	Lieut Murray
"	"	" C Group	do	Lieut Murray
Fri.	1145-1245	A	Gen Knowledge.	Lieut Murray
"	"	" C Group	do	" "
"	"	B	do	Sergt Firth
"	"	" C Group	do	" "
Sat.	1145-1245	A. & B.	Debate.	All Instructors

(Sgnd) Dennis. Whiteside.
Education Officer.

www.ingramcontent.com/pod-product-compliance
Lightning Source LLC
Chambersburg PA
CBHW081422160426
43193CB00013B/2176